FIRST APPEARANCE: Avengers Vol. 1 #66 (1969)

HISTORY: Adamantium is a virtually indestructible steel alloy named after the fabled metal Adamantine of Greek mythology. The metal has its origins in the work of American metallurgist Doctor Myron MacLain during World War II when the U.S. government assigned him to military research and development. Through a metallurgic accident, MacLain created the indestructible Vibranium-steel compound that was used to create the shield used by the super-soldier Captain America. MacLain spent decades attempting to duplicate the process, and although unsuccessful, he instead created True Adamantium in the 1960s.

Extraordinarily expensive to produce, Adamantium is created through the mixing of certain chemical resins whose exact composition is a closely guarded government secret. For eight minutes after the resins are mixed, Adamantium can be molded if kept at a temperature of 1,500 degrees Fahrenheit. Its extremely stable molecular structure prevents it from being molded further, even if the temperature remains high enough to keep it in liquefied form. Hardened Adamantium can only be altered by rearrangement of its cellular structure. Given sufficient mass, Adamantium could survive a direct hit from a nuclear weapon or a blow from the most powerful superhuman. The only known substance able to pierce Adamantium is the compound known as Antarctic Vibranium, also called "anti-metal."

The U.S. government has shared the secret of Adamantium's composition with certain allies, though the information has fallen into unauthorized hands. Attempts by the former Soviet Union to reproduce the metal resulted in the creation of Carbonadium, a weaker yet far [...] retractable coils [...] Due to the prob[...] have resorted to the use of a somewhat [...] Secondary Adamantium, which was once used to coat the sentient computer named F.A.U.S.T.

The Japanese scientist Lord Dark Wind was the first to propose a procedure by which Adamantium could be bonded to a human skeleton. Dark Wind's theory was practiced by the clandestine Weapon X Program who subjected their former mutant operative, Wolverine, to the procedure. Wolverine's mutant healing factor allowed him to survive the process and induced a molecular change in the metal, transforming it into a wholly new metal, named Adamantium Beta, that does not inhibit the biological processes of bone.

Dark Wind himself performed a similar procedure on the assassin Bullseye to replace some of his bones, while Weapon X repeated their earlier success with the feral mutant Sabretooth. A similar process was performed on the mutant mercenary Cyber to lace his skin with Adamantium, and the cyborg Donald Pierce once used the metal to rebuild his then-shattered form. The metal has also been used to coat certain robots, such as the superhuman-hunting TESS-One, and to forge others such as the megalomaniacal Ultrons.

The Adametco company in New Jersey has developed a procedure to coat objects with a thin layer of Adamantium. As a result, the plant has been targeted by such costumed criminals as the Overrider and the Absorbing Man, who sought to obtain Adamantium for their personal use.

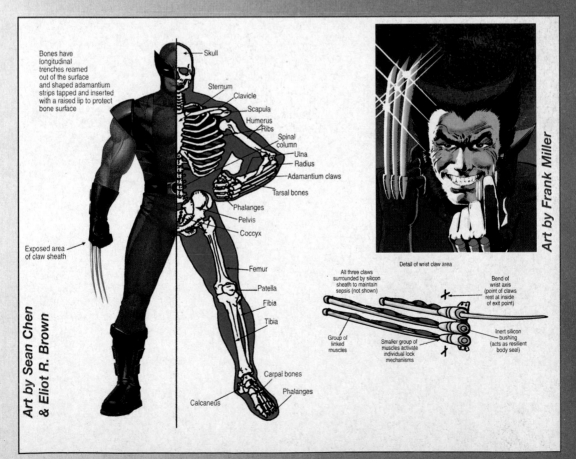

Art by Sean Chen & Eliot R. Brown

Art by Frank Miller

Bones have longitudinal trenches reamed out of the surface and shaped adamantium strips tapped and inserted with a raised lip to protect bone surface

Skull
Sternum
Clavicle
Scapula
Humerus
Ribs
Spinal column
Ulna
Radius
Adamantium claws
Tarsal bones
Phalanges
Pelvis
Coccyx
Femur
Patella
Fibia
Tibia
Carpal bones
Phalanges
Calcaneus

Exposed area of claw sheath

Detail of wrist claw area

All three claws surrounded by silicon sheath to maintain sepsis (not shown)

Bend of wrist axis (point of claws rest at inside of exit point)

Group of linked muscles

Smaller group of muscles activate individual lock mechanisms

Inert silicon bushing (acts as resilient body seal)

REAL NAME: Warren Kenneth Worthington III
KNOWN ALIASES: Formerly Angel, Avenging Angel
IDENTITY: Publicly known
OCCUPATION: Adventurer, teacher, chairman & principal stockholder of Worthington Industries; former terrorist, vigilante
CITIZENSHIP: U.S.A. (no criminal record)
PLACE OF BIRTH: Centerport, Long Island, New York
KNOWN RELATIVES: Warren Kenneth Sr. (grandfather, deceased), Warren Kenneth Jr. (father, deceased), Kathryn (mother, deceased), Burtram "Burt" (Dazzler, paternal uncle), unnamed cousin
GROUP AFFILIATION: X-Men, Mutantes Sans Frontières; formerly Secret Defenders, X-Factor/X-Terminators, Horsemen of Apocalypse, Defenders, Death's Champions, Champions of Los Angeles
EDUCATION: College degree from Xavier's School for Gifted Youngsters
FIRST APPEARANCE: X-Men #1 (1963)

HISTORY: Born into an extremely wealthy family, young Warren attended a prestigious East Coast boarding school where he roomed with Cameron Hodge. Warren's life changed forever the day he began sprouting wings from his shoulder blades, and he hid them under his clothes. Later, when fire struck his dormitory, Warren discovered while escaping that his wings enabled him to fly. Donning a blond wig and long nightshirt to disguise himself as an anonymous "angel," Warren saved the other students. Warren soon became the costumed crime-fighting Avenging Angel and attracted the attention of Professor Xavier, who recruited him as a founding member of the heroic, mutant X-Men team. After the young telepath Jean Grey joined the X-Men, Warren was instantly attracted to her. Eventually realizing that Jean loved their teammate Cyclops, Warren stopped pursuing her. Soon after, Warren rekindled his old college flame Candy Southern and the pair became inseparable. After his father was killed by agents of the criminal Dazzler, Warren investigated and was shocked to learn that the Dazzler was his uncle Burt, who had been using his brother's company as a cover for his crimes. In the ensuing battle, Warren dropped the Dazzler from a great height and presumed him dead. Burt survived and plotted to marry Warren's mother Kathryn in an effort to secure the family fortune. Furthermore, Burt had arranged for Kathryn to be secretly, gradually poisoned. Warren and the X-Men foiled Burt's plan, though too late to save Kathryn.

When the sentient island Krakoa captured the X-Men, Professor X assembled a second squad of X-Men to rescue them. After this, most of the original students — including Warren — left the team. Warren inherited his family fortune and used a portion of it to fund a Los Angeles-based super-team, the Champions. Warren revealed to the general public that he was the Angel, though his connection to Xavier's school remained secret. After the Champions disbanded, Warren eventually rejoined the X-Men, but his constant clashes with Wolverine soon led him to quit. After declining the first of two invitations to join the Avengers, Angel teamed with Spider-Man, Ka-Zar and the X-Men to defeat Sauron and the Savage Land Mutates; helped the Avengers battle his rampaging ex-Champions teammate Ghost Rider (Johnny Blaze); defeated his French counterpart Le Peregrine during the Grandmaster's Contest of Champions; and befriended the new Dazzler, mutant singer Alison Blaire, whom he romantically pursued for a time. Later, Angel joined the Defenders when that group reorganized as a more formal team under the guidance of his fellow X-Men graduate Beast. Angel served as financier of the new group, which was managed for a time by his girlfriend Candy, but they disbanded after most of its members seemingly died in battle with the Dragon of the Moon.

Angel then reunited with the other original X-Men in forming X-Factor, an organization that posed as mutant hunters but secretly helped fellow mutants. Warren's old friend Hodge was employed as X-Factor's public relations manager, but he had come to hate mutants, and he secretly used X-Factor's resources to fuel anti-mutant sentiment. Soon after, Warren's status as X-Factor's secret financial backer was leaked to the media, causing great controversy. During the Marauders' massacre of the subterranean Morlocks, Warren's wings were damaged by the Marauder Harpoon. Warren was hospitalized, and Hodge tricked the doctors into needlessly amputating his wings. Unaware of his friend's manipulation, Warren named Hodge beneficiary of his assets. With Warren deeply depressed after the loss of his wings, his break-up with Candy, and the controversy surrounding X-Factor, Hodge sabotaged Warren's plane in an attempt to kill him and create the appearance of suicide. Though the world believed him dead, Warren was rescued by the eternal mutant Apocalypse, who offered to restore his wings. Desperate, Warren agreed, and through technological and genetic manipulation, which turned his skin blue, he was given razor-sharp metal wings. Warren became Apocalypse's Horseman Death, but after being tricked into believing he had killed Iceman, he was eventually able to break Apocalypse's programming. Warren then hunted down Hodge, who had kidnapped Candy. In the ensuing clash, Hodge killed Candy and Warren decapitated Hodge. Warren subsequently rejoined X-Factor as Archangel, and soon saved the life of policewoman Charlotte Jones. The two became romantically involved, helping Warren reclaim his humanity.

Death. Warren then returned to the X-Men as a reservist, his responsibilities as head of Worthington Industries taking precedence. Ending his relationship with Psylocke, Warren later committed himself to the X-Men full-time, becoming team leader.

After Professor X was publicly exposed as a mutant, Warren took a more public role in his business activities, speaking to the G8 summit about mutants in the world economy. When the X-Men were captured by the plant-like mutant Black Tom Cassidy, Warren's skin reverted to normal after Tom drained some of his life-force.

Following an attack on the various heroic mutant teams by agents of the island nation Genosha, Warren learned that Hodge had survived, having bargained with a demon that granted him eternal life, but Hodge was ultimately defeated by the heroes. After X-Factor's members rejoined the X-Men, a mutual attraction developed between Warren and his teammate Psylocke. During this period, Warren teamed with Spider-Man, the New Warriors, the Avengers and other heroes to battle Darkling, whose Darkforce temporarily corrupted and controlled Archangel and other morally conflicted heroes before Darkling's defeat. The mystic Dr. Druid later tricked Archangel and Iceman into participating in a Secret Defenders mission that pitted them against old Champions foe Swarm, who was driven off before the duo ever learned who had manipulated them. Having inherited Club membership from his father, Warren declined an offer from the Club's then-Black King Shinobi Shaw to join its Inner Circle as the White King. Following a savage attack by the feral mutant Sabretooth, Warren and Psylocke, who had since become lovers, left the X-Men for a short time to recuperate. During this time, Warren's metallic wings molted, revealing that his original, feathered wings had grown back underneath. Later, when Professor X disbanded the X-Men in an attempt to ferret out an alien impostor, Warren joined an ad-hoc team of X-Men to help the young mutant Mannites battle Apocalypse's latest Horseman

Subsequently recovering from his injuries, Warren underwent a secondary mutation that gave his blood healing properties. When Xavier Institute student Husk uncovered corruption within Worthington Industries, she and Warren encountered the mutant werewolves the Dominant Species, whose leader, Maximus Lobo, claimed to have been the one who killed Warren's father. When Husk was severely injured by the werewolves, Warren used his newfound power to save her life, and the pair soon became romantically involved. After Cyclops became co-headmaster of the Institute, he asked Warren to establish a high-profile charity to improve mutantkind's image. Inspired by Robert A. Heinlein's story, "The Menace from Earth," Warren established "Wings over the World," a recreation center wherein visitors don artificial wings and fly by means of anti-gravity. Warren later also established "Mutantes Sans Frontières," a global outreach organization that sends trained mutant volunteers to places where the X-Men have no official presence. Setting up office in Zanzibar, Warren and Husk became involved in an attempt by the White Queen Courtney Ross to destabilize the country by employing the mercenary Viper and the Weaponeers. Alongside the country's President — who was secretly the superhero Askari — and Genoshan reinforcements, the heroes managed to repel the invaders.

HEIGHT: 6'
WEIGHT: 150 lbs.
EYES: Blue
HAIR: Blond

SUPERHUMAN POWERS: Archangel has fully feathered wings that span 16' and have a very flexible skeletal structure. He can fly by flapping his wings, and can reach speeds of up to 150 mph. Though he generally flies below the height of clouds at 6,500 feet, Archangel can reach a height of 10,000 feet with little effort. His wings are strong enough to carry aloft at least 200 pounds in addition to his own body weight. Archangel's entire anatomy is adapted for flight, having hollow bones; a body virtually devoid of fat, granting him enhanced proportionate muscle strength; eyes that can withstand high-speed winds; enhanced eyesight enabling him to see at distances far greater than the average human; and a special respiratory membrane that extracts oxygen from the air at extreme velocities and altitudes. Since his secondary mutation, Archangel can heal fatal injuries and cure most known diseases at an accelerated speed by mixing his blood with that of the victims, so long as they have a compatible blood type.

After genetic alteration by Apocalypse, Archangel's feathers were composed of a razor-sharp organic steel-like material. He could expel these feathers at great speed and with

tremendous force, enabling them to pierce even steel. The feathers were tipped with a paralyzing chemical generated by his body to which he was immune. He also briefly possessed the ability to convert his life-force into solid light to form a pair of energy wings.

ABILITIES: Archangel is a skilled combatant, especially in aerial hand-to-hand combat. He is also a talented businessman whose wealth ranks him in the lower part of the Fortune 500 list.

PARAPHERNALIA: Archangel often wears a harness to help conceal his wings underneath his clothes. When blue-skinned, Archangel used a holographic image inducer to grant him a normal appearance. For a short time he wielded the Soulsword of the Exile Magik. As the Avenging Angel, he carried a gun loaded with knockout gas pellets.

POWER GRID	1	2	3	4	5	6	7
INTELLIGENCE							
STRENGTH							
SPEED							
DURABILITY							
ENERGY PROJECTION							
FIGHTING SKILLS							

BEAST

REAL NAME: Henry "Hank" P. McCoy
KNOWN ALIASES: Formerly Kreature, Mutate #666
IDENTITY: Publicly known
OCCUPATION: Adventurer, former biochemist, college lecturer
PLACE OF BIRTH: Dunfee, Illinois
CITIZENSHIP: United States of America with no criminal record
MARITAL STATUS: Single
KNOWN RELATIVES: Sadie McCoy (grandmother), Edna McCoy (mother), Norton McCoy (father). Robert McCoy (uncle)
GROUP AFFILIATION: X-Men, formerly X-Treme X-Men, X-Factor, Defenders, Avengers, Rejects
EDUCATION: Ph. D. Biochemistry

HISTORY: While working at a nuclear power plant, Norton McCoy was exposed to massive amounts of radiation that affected his genes. As a result, Norton's son, Henry "Hank" McCoy, was born a mutant who showed the signs of his being different from birth with his unusually large hands and feet.

As a youth, Hank's freakish appearance was the subject of much ridicule from his classmates, earning him the nickname of "beast". However, one classmate, Jennifer Nyles, came to know the real Hank after he began tutoring her in biology. On the night of the junior prom, Jennifer insisted that Hank accompany her as her date, and stood up for him after he was teased.

In his senior year, Hank's superhuman agility and athletic prowess earned him recognition as a star football player. During one game, Hank easily stopped a trio of robbers who were attempting to escape across the football field. The villain named the Conquistador noticed his efforts, kidnapping Hank's parents in an attempt to coerce the young mutant into working for him. The X-Men soon arrived and defeated the villain, and Hank was invited by Professor Charles Xavier to join the team of teenage mutant heroes and enroll in the Xavier School for Gifted Youngsters. Unable to resist the temptation of a private institution that could offer him limitless academic opportunities, Hank accepted.

A brilliant student, Hank completed his doctoral studies under Xavier's tutelage, and finally graduated from the Xavier School to take a position at the Brand Corporation as a genetic researcher under Doctor Carl Maddicks. During one of his experiments, Hank discovered the hormonal extract that causes genetic mutation and went to inform Maddicks of his findings. However, Maddicks was secretly plotting to steal top-secret government documents, and Hank took it upon himself to stop Maddicks. In order to disguise his appearance, Hank took the hormonal extract and underwent radical physical changes that enhanced his agility and strength – as well as causing him to grow fangs, pointed ears, and fur all over his body. When he stayed too long in this state, Hank found he could not return to his original form. He was now a beast in fact as well as in name. At first, he tried to hide his mutation with a latex mask and gloves, but later learned to accept his new appearance.

After receiving his doctorate in genetics and being considered one of the world's experts on mutations and evolutionary human biology, despite never having earned a Nobel Prize or been invited to join the National Academy of Sciences, Hank left Brand and applied to join the ranks of Earth's Mightiest Heroes in the Avengers. Initially accepted as a probationary member, Hank soon proved his worth and was granted full membership. During his time with the team he revealed his identity to the public in the hope that his status as an Avenger would help ease human/mutant tensions.

Following a restructuring of the Avengers, Hank left and became involved with the team of adventurers known as the Defenders which he soon reorganized into a more formal and cohesive unit, bringing in his former X-Men teammates Iceman and Angel. Following the apparent death of several of the Defenders, Hank reunited with the other four original X-Men to form X-Factor, an organization that intended to seek out and aid other mutants under the pretense of hunting down those perceived menaces to society. Shortly after the formation of X-Factor, Hank was captured by Maddicks, who sought to experiment on Hank in an attempt to find a "cure" for his son's own mutancy. However, the serum Hank was given caused him to revert to his original human appearance. Soon after, Hank first met television anchorwoman Trish Tilby, who was investigating X-Factor.

During an attack on New York by the eternal mutant Apocalypse and his Four Horsemen, Hank was stricken with a virus that sapped his intellect and increased his strength every time he exerted himself physically. The more Hank used his strength, the stronger he got, but the less intelligent he became. Finally, to save his friend Iceman from the deadly kiss of the mutant named Infectia, Hank intervened and was himself affected, the result of which returned him to his blue-furred form and restored his intellect. Soon after, Hank and Trish began seeing each other romantically; however her work often intruded on their relationship and the pair ultimately called it off.

After X-Factor disbanded, Hank returned to the ranks of the X-Men and became the team's resident technological and medical genius, working on everything from advanced alien technology to the deadly mutant-killing Legacy Virus. Hank also continued his on/off relationship with Trish until she released information on the Virus to the public, which caused hysteria that culminated in the beating to death of a young mutant.

During his tenure with the X-Men, Beast was lured into a trap and replaced in the ranks of the X-Men by the Dark Beast, an alternate-reality version of himself. Sealed behind a brick wall, Hank was nearly about to give up when his water tube broke and spurted, revealing the grooves of a trap door in his cell. Energized by hope, Beast broke his restraints and escaped with the aid of the new government-sponsored X-Factor team.

Hank returned to the X-Men in time to aid the team against the threat of the powerful psionic creature known as Onslaught. After the battle, Hank met with Trish and apologized for his previous harsh treatment of her. She forgave him and the pair renewed their relationship.

Hank eventually took an extended leave of absence from the X-Men to work on a cure for the Legacy Virus, which he ultimately found thanks to his implementing the work of his former colleague, the late Moira MacTaggart. Soon after, Hank joined Storm's team of X-Treme X-Men in their quest for the diaries of the late mutant seer Destiny. Almost killed in the team's first battle with the enhanced human named Vargas, Hank's life was saved by his teammate Tessa who used a heretofore-unseen power to accelerate his mutation to a new level.

Hank returned to Xavier's mansion to recuperate and mutated further, becoming bulkier, heavier, and taking on a more lionesque appearance. Forced to relearn fine motor control over his body, Hank once again served as the team's resident genius, as well as an active teacher of dozens of young mutants at the renamed Xavier Institute of Higher Learning.

Unable to deal with his latest mutation, Trish called Hank and ended their relationship over the phone. Soon after, Hank was beaten into a coma by a student possessed by Professor Xavier's malevolent twin Cassandra Nova, who herself had possessed Xavier's body. Hank recovered in time to expose her plans and Cassandra was ultimately defeated, but not before she had exposed her brother Charles to the world as a mutant, forever changing life at the Xavier mansion for the X-Men.

POWER GRID

	1	2	3	4	5	6	7
INTELLIGENCE							
STRENGTH							
SPEED							
DURABILITY							
ENERGY PROJECTION							
FIGHTING SKILLS							

CURRENT MEMBERS: Avalanche (Dominic Petros), Black Tom (Tom Cassidy), Exodus (Bennet du Paris), Mammomax, Sabretooth (Victor Creed)

FORMER MEMBERS: Angel (Angel Salvadore), Astra, Basilisk, Beak (Barnell Bohusk), Beast (Henry McCoy), Blob (Fred Dukes), Burner (Byron Calley), Dark Beast (Henry McCoy), Destiny (Irene Adler), Ernst, Esme, Ever, Fatale (Pamela), Havok (Alex Summers), Martha Johansson, Juggernaut (Cain Marko), Lifter (Ned Lanthrop), Lorelei, Magneto (imposter), Magneto (Magnus), Mastermind (Jason Wyngarde), Mastermind (Martinique Jason), Mimic (Calvin Rankin), Mystique (Raven Darkhölme), Nocturne (Talia Wagner), Peeper (Peter Quinn), Phantazia (Eileen Harsaw), Post (Kevin Tremain), Professor X (Charles Xavier), Pyro (St. John Allerdyce), Quicksilver (Pietro Maximoff), Random (Marshall Stone III), Rogue (Anna Marie), Sauron (Karl Lykos), Scarlet Witch (Wanda Maximoff), Shocker (Randall Darby), Slither (Aaron Solomon), Toad (Mortimer Toynbee), Unus (Angelo Unuscione), X-Man (Nate Grey)

BASE OF OPERATIONS: Worldwide

FIRST APPEARANCE: X-Men #4 (1964)

HISTORY: The Brotherhood of Mutants is a group dedicated to the cause of mutant superiority over humans. Throughout its various incarnations, the Brotherhood's agenda has gravitated towards either subjugating the human race to the will of mutants or eradicating humanity altogether. Magneto formed the Brotherhood of Evil Mutants, including Astra, Toad, Quicksilver, Scarlet Witch, and Mastermind, shortly after the public debut of the X-Men. After a falling out with Astra that led to her quitting the team, Magneto had the Brotherhood initiate an attack upon humans that was thwarted by the X-Men. Magneto then attempted to recruit the thunder god Thor into his Brotherhood, but Thor refused. The Blob was the next candidate for recruitment, but ultimately declined to join after seeing the way Magneto mistreated his followers. Mastermind then sought to recruit Unus the Untouchable; however, he was blackmailed by the X-Men into declining the offer in exchange for reversing his then-amplified powers. During an encounter with the enigmatic Stranger, Magneto and the Toad were captured and taken to the Stranger's homeworld, shortly after which Quicksilver and the Scarlet Witch joined a revamped version of the Avengers led by Captain America.

After a tenure with the subversive organization Factor Three (intended to become a third major world power), Blob, Mastermind, and Unus banded together as a new Brotherhood. Following a failed attempt to settle the score with the X-Men, the trio were able to make the Beast believe he had killed the Avenger Iron Man and manipulated him into joining until he realized the truth and single-handedly defeated them. Eventually returning to Earth, Magneto re-formed the Brotherhood with Toad, Blob, Mastermind, Unus, and the Savage Land Mutate Lorelei to assist him in the creation of a being with unlimited power that he dubbed Alpha, the Ultimate Mutant. In an encounter with the Defenders, the rapidly evolving Alpha unleashed his powers, reducing the Brotherhood to a state of infancy. Subsequently restored to adulthood by Eric the Red of the alien Shi'ar race, Magneto formed a new Brotherhood comprising Lifter, Burner, Shocker, Slither, and Peeper. When they failed to capture the mutant with two bodies known as Mister One and Mister Two, Magneto abandoned this team, though they remained together as the Mutant Force and later temporarily became the Resistants.

The mutant shapeshifter Mystique formed her own Brotherhood of Evil Mutants, recruiting Blob, Pyro, Avalanche, Destiny, and her own foster daughter, Rogue. Mystique sent the Brotherhood against Carol Danvers, then known as Ms. Marvel (later Binary and Warbird), which ultimately led to Rogue absorbing and retaining Danvers' powers and memories. Mystique intended for the Brotherhood to assassinate then-anti-mutant Senator Kelly, but they met defeat after the

X-Men intervened and were incarcerated. Rogue freed the imprisoned members from captivity, but the male members were quickly recaptured after a struggle with the Galadorian Spaceknight named Rom. Mystique then sought to recruit the Dire Wraith/human half-breed Hybrid as a member; however, he proved too powerful for her to control, and the "Sisterhood" eventually aided Rom in temporarily destroying Hybrid. Subsequent efforts to target the X-Man Angel led to an encounter with Alison Blaire, the Dazzler, with whom Rogue quickly developed a fierce rivalry until Dazzler definitively defeated her.

Rogue eventually left the Brotherhood to seek help with controlling her powers and joined the X-Men. Soon after, Mystique's Brotherhood gained the support of the United States government by apprehending Magneto and became the first government-sponsored mutant team, Freedom Force. The team's ranks swelled with the addition of vigilantes Crimson Commando, Silver Sabre, and Stonewall, as well as the interdimensional Spiral and Julia Carpenter, the new Spider-Woman. Freedom Force conducted various missions for the government, ultimately losing both Destiny and Stonewall in battle against the cyborg Reavers on Muir Island. After Mystique, Spiral, and Spider-Woman left the team, the remaining members were sent on a mission to rescue nuclear physicist Harvey Kurtzman from captivity in Kuwait. The operation went awry after they encountered the Arab super team Desert Sword. During the battle, Pyro killed both Kurtzman and Desert Sword operative Veil, Super Sabre was beheaded by Aminedi, and Crimson Commando was critically injured. Avalanche and Commando managed to escape alongside a squad of American soldiers, leaving Blob and Pyro to be captured.

Eventually the Toad sought to form a new Brotherhood, recruiting Blob, Pyro, Sauron, and Phantazia, and allied with the Morlocks to take down the mutant strike team X-Force. During the battle, both Sauron and the Morlocks' leader Masque were seemingly killed; however both later resurfaced, with Sauron rejoining the Brotherhood prior to a failed attack on X-Factor. Following a clash with the crime-fighting Darkhawk and the enigmatic Sleepwalker over the interdimensional mutant Portal, Toad's Brotherhood disbanded.

Soon after, X-Factor's then-leader Havok sought to expose the clandestine genetic experiments of the alternate reality Dark Beast. He created the impression that he had decided Xavier's dream was futile and re-formed the Brotherhood as a proactive mutant team against humanity, abandoning the "evil mutants" tag. With the telepathic Ever, Havok faked an assassination attempt on Daily Bugle publisher J. Jonah Jameson which was stopped by the X-Men. Havok then recruited the Dark Beast and his assassin Fatale into the Brotherhood in order to keep closer watch on the Dark Beast's activities, as well as Nate Grey. After Havok's true motives were revealed and the Dark Beast was defeated, Havok disbanded the Brotherhood and returned to X-Factor.

The next incarnation of the team came when Professor Xavier was imprisoned by the government-sanctioned Operation: Zero Tolerance. Freed by a new Brotherhood of Mutants led by the Blob and consisting of Toad, Post and Mimic, Xavier agreed to train them to better their chances of survival against the then-sentient computer Cerebro. After Cerebro

was defeated by Xavier, the Brotherhood was employed by Mystique to recover the remains of X-51, the Machine Man, after which she reorganized the team. Mystique recruited some of her old teammates along with Sabretooth, Toad, Post, and Mastermind (Martinique Jason) with a view to launching another assassination attempt on then-presidential candidate Senator Kelly. As Mystique, Sabretooth and Toad created a diversion by attacking the Muir Island Research Facility, Post, Blob, Avalanche, and Mastermind targeted Kelly. In response, the X-Men split into two groups to stop the Brotherhood but were unable to prevent the destruction of Muir. They would have been too late to save Kelly if not for the timely arrival of former Brotherhood member Pyro, who was in the final stages of the deadly mutant-killing Legacy Virus and sought to redeem himself before he died. Pyro sacrificed his life to incinerate Post, thus preventing Kelly's death. Despite this selfless act, Kelly was ultimately killed by an anti-mutant protester who believed him to be a race traitor.

Following Mystique's imprisonment, many of the Brotherhood members were recruited by former X-Man Banshee into the paramilitary X-Corps group, leaving the way clear for a terrorist coalition to claim the name of The Brotherhood. Formed by mutant activists Hoffman and Marshal, this militant group engaged in worldwide terrorist activities before Marshal ultimately quit over Hoffman's growing hunger for power. Marshal became a government agent intent on taking Hoffman down and managed to convince three captured Brotherhood members to sell Hoffman out in exchange for their freedom. Ultimately, this Brotherhood was dismantled after many of its members, including Hoffman, were killed during a failed assassination attempt on Doop of the celebrity mutant group X-Force.

After infiltrating Xavier's school in the guise of the mutant healer Xorn, a Magneto imposter adopted the Institute's special class of students — Basilisk, Ernst, Martha Johansson, Beak, and Angel — as his Brotherhood. Joined by Toad and Esme of the Stepford Cuckoos, the faux Magneto attempted a hostile takeover of Manhattan. However, his inability to control the resulting chaos resulted in the fracturing of the Brotherhood after he inadvertently killed Basilisk and was himself decapitated by Wolverine.

Recently the Brotherhood was reorganized by Magneto's former Acolyte Exodus, who recruited Black Tom, Avalanche, Sabretooth, Mammomax, and Nocturne for an all-out attack on the X-Men. The Brotherhood planned their attack based on inside knowledge provided by an apparent turncoat X-Man, the Juggernaut; however, he was revealed to be a mole planted by the X-Men. After a pitched battle, Exodus' Brotherhood was defeated when the X-Man Xorn created a black hole from the microscopic star in his brain which pulled them in and closed behind them. The final fate of this incarnation of the Brotherhood is yet to be revealed.

Art by John Byrne

CALLISTO

REAL NAME: Unrevealed
KNOWN ALIASES: None
IDENTITY: No dual identity
OCCUPATION: Operative of Professor X; formerly arena fighter, bodyguard, Morlock leader
CITIZENSHIP: Unrevealed
PLACE OF BIRTH: Unrevealed
KNOWN RELATIVES: None
GROUP AFFILIATION: Genoshan Excalibur; formerly the Arena, Morlocks
EDUCATION: Unrevealed
FIRST APPEARANCE: Uncanny X-Men #169 (1983)

HISTORY: Well over twenty years ago, having lived among normal humans and earned "scars to show how dumb a mistake that was," the woman now called Callisto discovered the huge tunnel network called the Alley beneath Manhattan. Aided by the mutant-detecting Caliban, the devoted Sunder and the treacherous Masque, she organized a community of mutant outcasts called the Morlocks. Unknown to Callisto, the Morlocks were being manipulated by the extradimensional sadist called the Dark Beast.

In recent years, Callisto, apparently driven to irrationality by her responsibilities, abducted the winged Angel (Warren Worthington III) as a consort. Angel's X-Men teammates invaded the Alley but were captured as well. The team's leader, Storm, challenged Callisto to trial by combat, almost killing her and winning the mantle of Morlock leader. Initially hating Storm, Callisto, de facto leader in Storm's absence, grew to respect the X-Men and their founder, Professor X, whose life she saved after he was beaten.

When most Morlocks were murdered by Mister Sinister's Marauders, the survivors were treated by Moira MacTaggart; in gratitude, Callisto appointed herself MacTaggart's bodyguard and assisted Cyclops against the mutant-hating Master Mold. However, she was captured by Masque, who had, via the young telepath Brain Cell, enslaved the remaining Morlocks. To taunt her, Masque restored Callisto's long-lost beauty, altered her memories, and then freed her in New York to be hunted down. However, Colossus protected Callisto, and Masque returned Callisto's scarred appearance before escaping. When Masque was believed dead, the remaining Morlocks went mad and attacked Callisto, who sought the X-Men's aid. However, Mikhail Rasputin, Colossus's brother, convinced Callisto to join him in leading the Morlocks to the Hill, a dimension of rapid time passage. There the survivors built a new society, but the younger generation escaped to Earth as the terrorist unit Gene Nation. Callisto again recruited the X-Men to stop her wayward charges, whom she later tried to rehabilitate in the Alley.

When the government anti-mutant persecution increased, Callisto and her protégé Marrow attacked official Henry Gyrich, but were held off by Spider-Man, who in turn helped battle Prime Sentinels. Severely wounded, Callisto was cared for by Marrow, but the Dark Beast manipulated her into departing. She resurfaced as a mutant gladiator in the mysterious Arena, her body given tentacles by a surviving Masque. However, when Storm was pressed into Arena performance, Callisto joined Storm and her allies to topple Masque. At Storm's request, Callisto joined Professor X's efforts rebuild the decimated nation Genosha. As a member of his informal inner circle, Excalibur, she has fought Trolls, the Weaponeers and other threats.

Callisto was recently de-powered during M-Day.

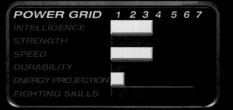

HEIGHT: 5'9"
WEIGHT: 165 lbs.
EYES: Blue
HAIR: Black

ABILITIES/ACCESSORIES: Callisto has heightened strength, agility and reflexes, augmented by her tentacles, which can adhere to any surface. Her senses are augmented. She is a natural-born leader, huntress, and fighter skilled in virtually every form of hand-to-hand combat; she frequently employs throwing knives.

POWER GRID	1	2	3	4	5	6	7
INTELLIGENCE							
STRENGTH							
SPEED							
DURABILITY							
ENERGY PROJECTION							
FIGHTING SKILLS							

HISTORY: Charles Xavier began to design his mutant-locating computer Cerebro early in his crusade to aid his fellow mutants, beginning work while he lived in Bombay, India, after being crippled by the extraterrestrial Lucifer. He completed his first model at his mansion in Westchester County, naming it "Cyberno." He first used Cyberno to locate the young mutant runaway Scott Summers. Pinpointing Summers' location, Cyberno also detected a second mutant, the criminal Jack O'Diamonds (Jack Winters). After rescuing Summers from Winters and recruiting him as Cyclops, the first member of the team of trainee mutants that became the X-Men, Xavier realized that an enhanced version of Cyberno would allow him to locate even more mutants. Refining the design, Xavier created a new version shortly before Jean Grey joined the X-Men as Marvel Girl, naming it Cerebro, from the Latin "cerebrum", meaning "the brain." The original Cerebro was simply a control panel built into Xavier's desk, to which Xavier later connected a radar-image beam that projected images of the mutants it detected, as well as a multi-frequency booster enabling Cerebro to pinpoint mutant locations which was connected using plastisthene tubing, an ultra-magnetic splicer and super-tensile cables. More additions followed, including a

ALIASES: The Founder, Cerebro Prime, Cyberno
OCCUPATION: Mutant locator
PLACE OF CREATION: Xavier's School for Gifted Youngsters, Salem Center, New York
CREATOR: Charles Xavier
GROUP AFFILIATION: Formerly led own X-Men team
FIRST APPEARANCE: X-Men #7 (1964)

tape recorder, visi-screen, a memory-erasing helmet, and an emergency circuit that would automatically activate Cerebro upon detecting a mutant signal. Cerebro soon grew to require a dedicated chamber within the mansion. Realizing the danger inherent in a subversive force gaining control of the device, Xavier installed numerous security protocols to help safeguard Cerebro. Xavier continued to upgrade the machine, even creating small portable versions that could pinpoint an individual mutant's location via telemetric communication with the parent unit. Following the X-Men mansion's destruction by the alien Sidri, it was rebuilt and its technological systems, including Cerebro, were upgraded with alien Shi'ar technology. The new Cerebro consisted of a powerful

Art by Jim Calafiore & Jack Kirby (inset)

Art by Frank Quitely

computer core, specialized wave-sensing components, and an interface helmet that could amplify its user's telepathic abilities. A second unit was subsequently installed at the Muir Island Research Center, run by Xavier's trusted friend Moira MacTaggart.

After the techno-organic alien Phalanx infiltrated the mansion and sought to access Cerebro's files, the X-Man Banshee was forced to initiate Cerebro's self-destruct sequence. Months later, Xavier finished rebuilding Cerebro; however, the computer detected a massive energy spike in northern New Jersey (caused by several mutants going wild on a train) immediately after initializing, and overloaded. The X-Man Bishop was then tasked with repairing Cerebro, noting that the advanced technology used in its design was the same as that in his own future time. When the X-Men were attacked by the government-sponsored Operation: Zero Tolerance anti-mutant taskforce, its leader, Bastion, confiscated the mansion's entire contents, including Cerebro. Bastion's Prime Sentinels attempted to interface with Cerebro, whereupon its security protocols engaged, downloading its central programming into the Prime Sentinels' neural network. Combined with Bastion's nanotechnology, Cerebro achieved sentience as Cerebro Prime.

Creating a nanotech body for itself, Cerebro set out to realize Xavier's dream through the ultimate fulfillment of its own program to find, catalogue, and store mutants. First, it had to overcome Bastion's nanotech programming, so it shaped itself into a facsimile of Xavier called "The Founder," and generated nanotech X-Men based on amalgams of its records. The Grey King (Addison Falk) was a power-dampening telepathic and telekinetic mutant based on Cyclops and Jean Grey; Rapture (Sister Joy) was a blue-skinned winged mutant combination of Archangel and Mystique; Chaos (Dan Dash) was an autistic mutant who could generate cosmic energy similar to Havok; Landslide (Lee Broder) was a massive, super-strong and agile mutant that resembled an amalgam of the Blob and the Beast; Crux (Cristal Lemieux) was a teenage French mutant with the ability to manipulate temperature extremes akin to Iceman and Sunfire; while Mercury possessed a liquid metal body.

These faux X-Men kidnapped Shadowcat, as Cerebro knew of her exceptional computer skills and believed she possessed the ability to save it. Thinking that Cerebro was the real Professor X, Kitty agreed to help. Cerebro and its X-Men then attempted to use a mutant-tracking satellite to catalogue all the mutants on the planet, but were stopped by the true X-Men. The rocket and the satellite were both destroyed, and the Founder abandoned its pretense of being Xavier. It reabsorbed the faux X-Men, then sought out Xavier, finding him at two locations simultaneously. To that end, Cerebro created two Cerebrite extensions of itself. One traveled to San Francisco where it faced a powerless Xavier alongside the Blob's Brotherhood of Mutants, while the other traveled

to Tajikinistan and found the Mannite Nina, who had imprinted Xavier's psi-pattern, and her guardian Renee Majcomb. Tracking Cerebro to its base in Florida, the X-Men were easily defeated. Finally, Xavier had Nina restore his powers, and using them in conjunction with her own, accessed Cerebro's nanotech mind and expanded its "consciousness" to the entire world. Cerebro's nanites, which it was planning to use to control all humans on the planet, were stopped and destroyed. Cerebro was overwhelmed by the unique individuality of each person and overloaded, expiring in its creator's arms.

Convinced that Cerebro was still a necessity, Xavier subsequently built a new version. Soon after, its files were accessed by X-51, the Machine Man, who was seeking a way to prevent his CPU from being corrupted by Sentinel programming. Cerebro was later significantly upgraded to consist of a large spherical chamber with a suspended walkway leading to the control console, command chair and interface helmet in the center. Recently, the Beast (Hank McCoy) adapted Xavier's original designs and built a more powerful version, which he dubbed "Cerebra." Originally an egg-shaped amplification chamber which housed a control chair and interface helmet, Cerebra was designed to boost the user's telepathic activity to a global range, representing mutant signatures as points of light on a virtual world map, with the height of each point indicating the relative power level of an individual mutant. Smaller versions of Cerebra were installed around the world in the offices of Xavier's X-Corporation. After the Institute's destruction by a mutant impersonating Magneto, Cerebra was redesigned using Cerebro's spherical chamber model. In this new configuration, Cerebra can not only locate and catalogue mutants, but can also holographically recreate an individual mutant's recent memories.

ABILITIES/ACCESSORIES: Cerebra's (and its predecessors') primary function is to detect and catalogue the world's mutants. The device constantly sweeps the globe by piggybacking pre-existing satellite projections in search of the aberrations in electromagnetic brainwave activity that are most often attributed to mutants. Various environmental factors, such as the degradation of the Earth's ozone layer, can limit the device's performance. Cerebra's computer systems can pinpoint a mutant's geographical location, roughly measure the mutant's power level, and even specify the mutant's identity if sufficient data exists within its systems. Cerebra has an extremely large storage capacity, having been upgraded from Cerebro's 500 petabyte capacity to a 150 exabyte volume. While Cerebra's performance is significantly improved when operated by a trained psi-sensitive mutant, it is also user-friendly to non-mutants with proper training. Those unskilled in its use place themselves at risk of suffering serious mental trauma, even death, due to the strain the device can place on the mind. Extended use of Cerebra can result in a low-grade REM sleep disruption.

HISTORY: Growing up on his parents' farm, Piotr Rasputin saw his older brother Mikhail become a cosmonaut. Mikhail was later discovered to be a latent mutant with energy warping powers, and to keep him secret the government faked his death. In later years, Piotr learned that he too was a mutant, and could transform his flesh into steel, but he was content to use his powers to help his fellow farmers. When a transformed Piotr rescued his sister Illyana from a runaway tractor, he was approached by Professor Charles Xavier, who was recruiting mutants for a new team of X-Men to help save his original students from the sentient island Krakoa. Dubbed Colossus by Xavier, Piotr reluctantly joined this new team, which freed the original X-Men and helped defeat Krakoa. After the battle, Piotr remained with the X-Men in America, though he found it difficult to adjust to living in a different culture.

When the X-Men visited the prehistoric Savage Land in Antarctica, Colossus saved some native women from a dinosaur. In return, the two surviving women, Nereel and Shakani, bade him join in a ritual to honor their fallen friend. Said ritual involved the creation of a new life, and though Piotr was initially reluctant, the two women persisted until he surrendered himself to their affections. Later, the X-Men were captured by the assassin Arcade, who brainwashed Colossus into believing he was the Proletarian, workers' hero of communist Russia, and turned him against his teammates. Colossus overcame this conditioning, and the X-Men soon faced the reality-manipulating mutant Proteus, who proved to be vulnerable to metal. Seizing upon this weakness, Colossus plunged his metal fists into the heart of Proteus' energy form, seemingly destroying him and taking Colossus' innocence along with him. Soon after, the X-Men recruited young mutant Kitty Pryde. Despite their initial shyness, a romance blossomed between her and Colossus. Later, Arcade's assistant Miss Locke kidnapped the X-Men's loved ones, including Illyana, to coerce the team into rescuing Arcade from the despotic Doctor Doom. The X-Men rescued them, and Illyana remained with her brother at Xavier's mansion. Eventually, Illyana was trapped in the demon-filled realm Limbo by its then-master, Belasco. She remained his captive for many years, though only moments had elapsed on Earth, and returned as the adolescent sorceress Magik.

Colossus and Kitty grew closer, finally admitting their feelings for one another. Colossus was among the X-Men forced by the godlike Beyonder to fight on his Battleworld. There, he fell in love with the healer Zsaji. After Colossus was killed by a cosmic-powered Doom, Zsaji gave her life to resurrect him. A heartbroken Colossus returned to Earth, ending his relationship with Kitty, though they remained friends. Colossus was later forced to take another life when the Marauders attacked the subterranean Morlocks. To save his teammate Nightcrawler, Colossus killed the Marauder Riptide; however, Riptide's attacks caused Colossus' bio-energy to leak from his metallic form like blood from a flesh wound. The X-Men's then-ally Magneto attempted to heal Colossus with his magnetic powers, but was only able to close the wounds, trapping Colossus in his metal state. After recuperating on Muir Isle, Colossus later rejoined the X-Men in opposing the mystic Adversary in Dallas. When the X-Men returned to the Savage Land after it had been razed by the giant alien Terminus, Colossus was reunited with Nereel. He met her son, Peter, unaware that the boy was the result of his earlier union with Nereel.

After a failed demonic invasion of New York, Illyana regressed in age. Colossus believed she would be safer away from the X-Men and sent her home to Russia while he returned to Australia with the team. Weary of seemingly endless battles, the X-Men entered the Siege Perilous, a mystic gateway that judged all who

REAL NAME: Piotr Nikolaievitch Rasputin
KNOWN ALIASES: Peter Rasputin, formerly Peter Nicholas, the Proletarian
IDENTITY: Secret
OCCUPATION: Adventurer; former artist, superintendent, student, farmer
CITIZENSHIP: U.S.A. (naturalized), formerly Russian
PLACE OF BIRTH: Ust-Ordynski Collective, near Lake Baikal, Siberia, Russia
KNOWN RELATIVES: Grigory Efimovich (great-grandfather, deceased), Elena (great-grandmother, deceased), Ivan (great-grand uncle, deceased), Grigory (grandfather, deceased), Nikolai (father, deceased), Alexandra (mother, deceased), Vladimir (uncle), unnamed aunt (deceased), unnamed uncle (deceased), Illyana Nikolievna (Magik, sister, deceased), Mikhail Nikolaievitch (brother), Peter Jr. (son), Larisa Mishchenko (cousin), Konstantin (cousin, deceased), Klara (cousin, deceased), Dimitriy (cousin, deceased)
GROUP AFFILIATION: X-Men; formerly Excalibur, Acolytes
EDUCATION: College level courses taken at Xavier's School for Gifted Youngsters, no degree
FIRST APPEARANCE: Giant-Size X-Men #1 (1975)

entered it and sent them to new lives. Colossus emerged virtually amnesiac, establishing a new identity as Peter Nicholas, a building superintendent who became a renowned artist. His idyllic existence ended when he was possessed by the psychic Shadow King and sent to kill Xavier. He was freed when Xavier erased the Peter Nicholas persona, restoring Colossus' true self, and he rejoined the X-Men. Soon after, the X-Men were pulled into a dimensional void where Colossus was reunited with Mikhail. The X-Men returned to Earth, bringing Mikhail with them; however, Mikhail's sanity had suffered due to his long years of isolation and he snapped, leading the Morlocks in an apparent mass suicide. Unknown to Colossus, Mikhail had actually teleported the Morlocks to an alternate dimension known as "the Hill."

Meanwhile, the Russian government invaded the Rasputin home, killing Colossus' parents and capturing Illyana, whom they sought to genetically accelerate to combat the threat of the mutant Soul Skinner. She was soon rescued by Colossus and came to live with him in America. Eventually, Illyana fell victim to the mutant-killing Legacy Virus, and a disillusioned Colossus abandoned Xavier's dream, joining Magneto's disciples, the Acolytes. After the destruction of Magneto's orbital base Avalon, Piotr searched for Kitty, then a member of the British super-team Excalibur. When he found Kitty kissing her then-boyfriend Pete Wisdom, Colossus nearly beat Wisdom to death in a jealous rage. Excalibur took responsibility for Colossus, and he came to accept his role with the team, serving as a valued member until they disbanded, after which Colossus rejoined the X-Men. When Xavier temporarily disbanded the X-Men in an effort to flush out an alien imposter, Colossus and his teammate Marrow set off on vacation, but were instead teleported to the Hill. There, Colossus freed Mikhail from the corrupting influence of a sentient energy being and took him back to Earth. Soon after, during a clash between the X-Men and the forces of Apocalypse, Mikhail used his powers to teleport Apocalypse's Horsemen to parts unknown.

Following the death of renowned geneticist Moira MacTaggart, the X-Men's resident scientist the Beast used her work to create a cure for the Legacy Virus; however, it could not be activated without emulating the manner in which the plague had first been discharged: through the death of an infected mutant. Having stood by, powerless, as his sister succumbed to the virus, Colossus injected himself with the formula. The serum caused his powers to flare, spreading the cure into Earth's atmosphere, claiming his life in the process. Colossus' body was supposedly cremated, and Kitty scattered the ashes over his Russian farmland home;

however, his body had secretly been stolen by Ord, an alien who had learned that an Earthly mutant would be responsible for destroying his world. Ord had come to Earth to declare war, but the spy agency S.W.O.R.D., a sub-division of S.H.I.E.L.D. handling extraterrestrial matters, was able to settle diplomatically with him. Ord had Colossus restored to life and imprisoned him for years while experimenting on him. Ultimately, Ord discovered the Legacy Virus cure still in Colossus' system and presented his findings to Benetech geneticist Doctor Kavita Rao, who modified it to create a "cure" for the "mutant condition." Learning of the cure, the X-Men went to Benetech to investigate. There, Kitty found Colossus alive and, after overcoming her initial shock, took him to aid the X-Men against Ord. Defeated, Ord was taken into custody, and Colossus returned home with the X-Men to adjust to his new lease on life.

Soon after, Colossus became involved in a mystery involving the deaths of several of his cousins — all of whom (like himself) were descended from the "doom of Old Russia," Grigori Rasputin — seemingly perpetrated by his brother Mikhail and the enigmatic geneticist, Mister Sinister.

HEIGHT: 6'6", (transformed) 7'5"
WEIGHT: 250 lbs., (transformed) 500 lbs.
EYES: Blue, (transformed) Silver
HAIR: Black

SUPERHUMAN POWERS: Colossus can transform his body tissue into an organic, steel-like substance that grants him superhuman strength and a high degree of imperviousness to injury. His armored form can withstand ballistic penetration as well as temperature extremes from 70° above absolute zero (-390° F) to approximately 9000° F. Colossus cannot become partially or selectively armored; his body is either entirely converted, or not at all. Even his eyes become steel-like.

Through an act of will, Colossus can transform virtually instantaneously into his armored state, and can remain in that form for an as yet undetermined amount of time. Once in his armored form, Colossus remains so until he consciously

wills himself back to normal. If he is rendered unconscious, however, he spontaneously reverts to his normal form. In his armored state, Colossus retains his normal human mobility, though his endurance and speed are enhanced. He does not need to breathe while transformed, but it is believed that he could not survive for long in a vacuum.

ABILITIES: Colossus is talented in drawing and painting.

POWER GRID

	1	2	3	4	5	6	7
INTELLIGENCE							
STRENGTH							
SPEED							
DURABILITY							
ENERGY PROJECTION							
FIGHTING SKILLS							

REAL NAME: Scott Summers
KNOWN ALIASES: Slim, formerly Slym Dayspring, Mutate #007, Eric the Red
IDENTITY: Publicly known
OCCUPATION: Co-headmaster of Xavier Institute for Higher Learning, adventurer, former student, radio announcer
PLACE OF BIRTH: Anchorage, Alaska
CITIZENSHIP: United States of America with no criminal record
MARITAL STATUS: Widowed (Jean Grey-Summers)
KNOWN RELATIVES: Philip Summers (grandfather), Deborah Summers (grandmother), Christopher Summers (Corsair, father), Katherine Anne Summers (mother, deceased), Alexander Summers (Havok, brother), Jack Winters (Jack O'Diamonds, former foster father), Jean Grey-Summers (Phoenix, wife, deceased), Madelyne Pryor-Summers (ex-wife, deceased), Nathan Christopher Summers (Cable, son), John Grey (father-in-law), Elaine Grey (mother-in-law), Sarah Grey-Bailey (sister-in-law, deceased), Aliya Jenskot (daughter-in-law, deceased), Tyler Dayspring (Genesis, grandson, deceased), Stryfe (clone son, deceased), Rachel Summers (Marvel Girl, alternate timeline daughter)
GROUP AFFILIATION: X-Men, formerly Astonishing X-Men, X-Factor
EDUCATION: College degree from Professor Xavier's School for Gifted Youngsters, post-graduate courses

HISTORY: Scott Summers was the first of two sons born to Major Christopher Summers, a test pilot for the U.S. Air Force, and his wife, Katherine. Christopher was flying his family home from vacation when a spacecraft from the interstellar Shi'ar Empire attacked their plane. To save their lives, Katherine pushed Scott and his brother, Alex, out of the plane with the only available parachute. Scott suffered a head injury upon landing, thus forever preventing him from controlling his mutant power by himself.

With their parents presumed dead, the authorities separated the two boys. Alex was adopted, but Scott remained comatose in a hospital for a year. On recovering, he was placed in an orphanage in Omaha, Nebraska that was secretly controlled by his future enemy, the evil geneticist Mr. Sinister.

As a teenager, Scott came into the foster care of Jack Winters, a mutant criminal known as the Jack O'Diamonds. After Scott began to suffer from severe headaches he was sent to a specialist, who discovered that lenses made of ruby quartz corrected the problem. Soon after, Scott's mutant power first erupted from his eyes as an uncontrollable blast of optic force. The blast demolished a crane, causing it to drop its payload toward a terrified crowd. Scott saved lives by obliterating the object with another blast, but the bystanders believed that he had tried to kill them and rallied into an angry mob. Scott fled, escaping on a freight train.

Winters sought to use Scott's newfound talents in his crimes, and physically abused the young boy when he initially refused. However, Scott's display of power had attracted the attention of the mutant telepath Professor Charles Xavier, who teamed up with F.B.I. agent Fred Duncan in their mutual attempt to find Scott. Xavier rescued Scott from Winters' clutches and enlisted him as the first member of the X-Men, a team of young mutants who trained to use their powers in the fight for human/mutant equality.

As Cyclops, Scott became deputy leader of the X-Men, and while he was a natural field general his social skills were lacking. Scott had fallen in love with his teammate Jean Grey, but his reserved demeanor prevented him from expressing his feelings for her for years. When Xavier's other original recruits left the fold following an encounter with the sentient island-being Krakoa, Cyclops stayed on as leader of the new team.

Shortly thereafter, the cosmic entity known as the Phoenix Force took Jean's place. When it committed suicide, Scott believed the love of his life had died and he left the X-Men. During his time away from the team, Scott met fishing boat captain Lee Forrester, who helped him work through his grief. Scott eventually returned to the X-Men whereupon he met Madelyne Pryor, a woman who bore an uncanny resemblance to Jean. Unaware that Madelyne was a clone of Jean created by Sinister, Scott fell in love with her and they were soon married. Madelyne fell pregnant and bore Scott a son they named Nathan Christopher.

When the real Jean emerged from suspended animation, Scott abandoned his wife and son and rejoined the other original X-Men in establishing a new team, X-Factor. During a demonic invasion of New York City, X-Factor and the X-Men fought against a super-powered and insane Madelyne. The invasion was thwarted after Madelyne perished in combat with Jean.

Later, the mutant warlord named Apocalypse infected baby Nathan with a techno-organic virus. To save his son's life, Scott had to allow a member of the Clan Askani to transport Nathan two millennia into the future, where it had been foreseen that he would deliver the world from Apocalypse's clutches. X-Factor disbanded soon after, and its members returned to the ranks of the X-Men. Scott and his long-time love Jean were married, and while on their honeymoon their spirits were taken into the timestream by the Clan Askani's matriarch. Arriving in the future, they inhabited new bodies, and raised Nathan for twelve years. When they returned to their own time and bodies, Nathan remained in the future and ultimately matured into his time's greatest hero: Cable.

Following Xavier's arrest for crimes committed as the evil psionic entity Onslaught, Scott assumed the role of leadership of the X-Men once more. Soon after, the government sponsored mutant-hunting operation known as "Zero Tolerance" took effect, and the villainous Bastion captured the X-Men. In his attempt to destroy mutantkind, Bastion placed a nanotech bomb inside Scott's body. The X-Men escaped, and the mutant doctor named Cecilia Reyes saved Scott's life. Scott and Jean then took a leave of absence from the X-Men for a period of recuperation.

Not long after returning to the team, Scott and Jean soon found themselves embroiled in Apocalypse's bid for cosmic power by assembling "The Twelve": a group of mutants who would determine the fate of their kind that counted Scott, Jean and Cable amongst their number. They were wired to a machine that would channel their awesome energies into Apocalypse, allowing him to absorb the body of the time-tossed powerful mutant teenager known as X-Man. As his teammates fell around him, a powerless Scott saved X-Man and merged with the would-be conqueror to create a new evil entity. Jean detected Scott's psyche inside Apocalypse and prevented the X-Men from destroying him, however, he was presumed dead by most of his teammates. Only Cable and Jean refused to believe Scott had perished. Investigating rumors he was alive, the pair found him in the birthplace of Apocalypse in Akkaba, Egypt, struggling to reassert his mind over the villain's psyche. Ultimately, Jean was able to physically rip Apocalypse's essence from Scott's body using her mental powers, and Cable destroyed it with his own telepathic powers.

Scott left for a small period of recuperation, during which he met and reconciled with his father. Afterwards, Scott returned to the X-Men, but his association with Apocalypse had given him a grimmer, more serious personality than ever before. As a result, many of his personal relationships became strained, including his marriage to Jean. Scott sought the counsel of his teammate Emma Frost, and the pair began a psychic affair. When Jean discovered Scott's betrayal, he left the X-Men in order to sort out the mess his life had become.

Following the outing of Professor X as a mutant to the world, his school, was rechristened the Xavier Institute of Higher Learning, and opened its doors to the mutant population at large, training and educating dozens of young new students to help them cope with their burgeoning abilities. After the death of his wife, Scott assumed the position of co-headmaster of the School alongside his new love, Emma.

PHYSICAL DESCRIPTION:

HEIGHT: 6'3"
WEIGHT: 195 lbs
EYES: Brown, glowing red when using powers
HAIR: Brown

DISTINGUISHING FEATURES: None

POWERS & ABILITIES:

STRENGTH LEVEL: Cyclops possesses the normal human strength of a man of his age, height, and build who engages in intensive regular exercise.

SUPERHUMAN POWERS: Cyclops possesses the mutant ability to project a beam of heatless, ruby-colored concussive force from his eyes, which act as interdimensional apertures between this universe and another. Cyclops's body constantly absorbs ambient energy, such as sunlight, from his environment into his body's cells, which allows him to open the apertures. Cyclops's mind generates a psionic field that is attuned to the forces that maintain the apertures. Because this field envelops his body, it automatically shunts the otherdimensional particles back into their point of origin when they collide with his body. Thus, his body is protected from the effects of the particles, and even the thin membranes of his eyelids are sufficient to block the emission of energy. The synthetic ruby quartz crystal used to fashion the lenses of Cyclops's eyewear is resonant to his mind's psionic field and is similarly protected.

The width of Cyclops's optic blast is focused by his mind's psionic field with the same autonomic function that regulated his original eyes' ability to focus. As Cyclops focuses, the size of the aperture changes and thus acts as a valve to control the flow of particles and the beam's relative power. The height of Cyclops's optic blast is controlled by his visor's adjustable slit. The beam's effective range is about 2,000 feet.

SPECIAL LIMITATIONS: Due to a head injury, Cyclops is unable to shut off his optic blasts at will and must therefore wear ruby quartz lenses to block the beams.

OTHER ACCESSORIES: The mask Cyclops wears to prevent random discharge is lined with powdered ruby quartz crystal. It incorporates two longitudinally mounted flat lenses that can lever inward providing a constantly variable exit slot. The inverted clamshell mechanism is operated by a twin system of miniature electrical motors. As a safety factor, there is a constant positive closing pressure provided by springs. The mask itself is made of high-impact cyclolac plastic. There is an overriding finger-operated control mechanism on either side of the mask, and normal operation is through a flat micro-switch installed in the thumb of either glove.

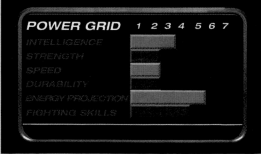

POWER GRID   1 2 3 4   5 6 7
INTELLIGENCE
STRENGTH
SPEED
DURABILITY
ENERGY PROJECTION
FIGHTING SKILLS

HISTORY: This reality diverged when Jean Grey received the Phoenix Force, rather than being replaced by it, and was not killed during the battle with the Imperial Guard. More world-wide changes followed the X-Men's failure to prevent Mystique and her Brotherhood of Evil Mutants from assassinating anti-mutant activist Senator Robert Kelly as humanity's fear of mutantkind changed to hatred. When another radical anti-mutant Senator, James Martin, was elected President, he passed a Mutant Affairs Control Act, which was quickly overturned as a wholesale violation of human rights; however, Martin was undeterred and formed Project Wideawake, a covert commission geared specifically towards dealing with the mutant situation.

The Project soon reactivated the giant mutant-hunting robot Sentinels and unleashed them on an unsuspecting mutant populace. The Sentinels, under the broad directive to protect humans against the menace of mutant domination of society, decided that the best way to carry out their programming was to assume control of Project Wideawake themselves, eliminating the moderating influence of their human masters. Within a few years, the Sentinels controlled all of North America. Mutants and non-mutant super-beings alike were rounded up in cattle cars and incarcerated in concentration camps where their powers were negated. Any that resisted, including the Avengers, the Fantastic Four, Spider-Man and Doctor Doom, were killed. The Sentinels established their control center in the Fantastic Four's former home, the Baxter Building.

Following an attack on the X-Men's mansion which killed their founder Charles Xavier, government troops captured survivor Rachel Summers, daughter of Cyclops and Jean Grey. Rachel was brainwashed by a scientist named Ahab, formerly Rory Campbell, into becoming the first of a new breed of mutant hunters called Hounds. With the telepathy she had inherited from her mother, Rachel proved to be a formidable tracker. Unknown to Ahab, Rachel stayed mindlocked with her targets at the moment of their death, fueling her shame and grief to the point where she was able to break free of her Hound programming. Resisting all attempts to reprogram her, Rachel was ultimately sent to a concentration camp where she was reunited with the remaining X-Men.

Meanwhile, Magneto sought aid in preventing the Hellfire Club from using the power of his daughter, the Scarlet Witch, to alter their world. Enlisting the help of Wolverine, the pair were able to free the Scarlet Witch; but during the attempt, Magneto's legs were shattered. As his daughter lay dying in his arms, he

CORE CONTINUUM DESIGNATION: Earth-811

SIGNIFICANT INHABITANTS: Ahab, Hounds, Magneto, President Martin, Nimrod, Resistance Coordination Executive (Albion, Arthur/Nigel Orpington-Smythe, Breeze, Dark Angel, Darkguard, Grace, Killpower, Motormouth, Pendragon's Knights, Tangerine, Union Jack), Franklin Richards, Rachel Summers, Sentinels, X-Men (Colossus/Piotr Rasputin, Shadowcat/Kate Pryde, Storm/Ororo Munroe, Wolverine/ James Howlett)

SIGNIFICANT LOCATIONS: Physically similar to Earth-616

FIRST APPEARANCE: X-Men #141 (1981)

promised to help the X-Men. Shortly after, he was captured and, along with Rachel and the X-Men, the heroes formed a plan to use Rachel's power of astral projection through time to go back and alter the past. With the help of Wolverine, who had avoided capture, the now-adult Kate Pryde smuggled in parts for a device that would override their power-negating collars. Once the device was complete, Rachel used her power to switch Kate's consciousness with that of her younger self, Kitty, who had only recently joined the X-Men in a time just prior to Kelly's assassination. As Kate attempted to convince the past X-Men of her plight, back in her time the X-Men sought to use their reclaimed powers to strike against the Sentinels' headquarters in the Baxter Building. Though they fought valiantly, all the X-Men except for Kate and Rachel were slain.

In the past, Kate convinced the X-Men to travel to Washington, where they prevented the Brotherhood from assassinating Kelly. With her task complete, Kate's consciousness returned to her own time where she discovered that her actions in the past had not changed her present. The Sentinels were still in control. Rachel sent her astral self into the past to discover that Kate's mission had taken her sideways to an alternate timeline (Earth-616). En route back to her own time, Rachel attracted the attention of the cosmic Phoenix Force entity, who initially mistook Rachel for her mother. Intrigued, the Force followed Rachel back to her time and witnessed her pass out from the strain of the journey. The Force revealed itself to Kate, who asked it to grant Rachel a chance for a fresh start.

The following day, Kate and Rachel infiltrated the Project Nimrod facility, intending to destroy it with a bomb. Just prior to detonation, the Force possessed Rachel, suppressing her memories of this horrendous time, and used her power to send her back to the Earth-616 of the past. The prototype Nimrod Sentinel detected this and followed Rachel before the bomb went off. Kate barely survived the explosion, but was captured by Ahab, who had learned of Rachel's time travel and sought to locate her. Kate's ability to disrupt electricity interfered with Ahab's probe, resulting in all of them being sent back in time. Kate and Ahab's Sentinel probe merged to become the robot Widget, while Ahab set about preventing any further rewriting of what was, for him, history.

Soon after, the adult Franklin Richards from Rachel's time appeared in the modern era of Earth-616. In the instant before his death at the hands of the Sentinels, Franklin had used his powers of dream-walking to transport his dream self to a time when he felt safe. When he arrived, the adult Franklin tapped into the power of his younger counterpart and Rachel's link to the Phoenix Force to give form to his desire. Tracked by Ahab, who hoped that Franklin would lead him to Rachel, Franklin sought help from his past family in the Fantastic Four and their allies in X-Factor. Ahab captured Rachel's father, Cyclops, and Franklin's mother, the Invisible Woman, and temporarily transformed them into Hounds to better assist him in his task. Ahab and his new Hounds easily captured Rachel and Franklin, but the rest of the Fantastic Four and X-Factor, along with the X-Men and Cable's New Mutants, managed to locate them. Their combined might proved enough to defeat the villain, who fled back to his own time, while the adult Franklin was forced to accept his own death lest he inadvertently harm Rachel and his younger self.

Much later, after Rachel's memory was restored, she sought to return to her own time to right the wrongs she had committed. With her then-teammates in Excalibur accompanying her, the heroes arrived in Britain in Rachel's timeline two years after she had escaped. By this time, the Sentinels had broadened their scope and were seeking to control the world, battling the Soviet

Super-Soldiers, the Asian Alliance Mega-Robots, and pockets of resistance in Europe and South America. Not content with controlling one Earth, the Sentinels were also planning to send Nimrod models to all tangential timelines in order to eradicate mutantkind. Together with the remaining members of the British Resistance Coordination Executive, the heroes managed to hold the Sentinels off long enough to let Rachel link Kate, in Widget's body, to the Sentinel Hierarchy's psybertronic brain. This allowed Kate to change the Sentinels' Prime Directive to ensure they would protect all life, putting an end to their genocidal plans.

To this day, the X-Men of the present remain haunted by their knowledge of the "Days of Future Past," knowing they must remain ever vigilant in their efforts lest they allow a similar future to eventuate.

In Earth-5700, an alternate version of this reality, the Director of the Weapon X Program, Malcolm Colcord, was ultimately responsible for unleashing the Sentinel assault on mutantkind. Other similarly Sentinel-dominated timelines include Earth-967, in which Rachel and Franklin's son grew up to be the powerful Hyperstorm; Earth-9620, the "Days of Future Tense" reality prophesied by Excalibur's Britannic (Brian Braddock); Earth-2600, in which Sabretooth of the Exiles lived for years while raising the powerful young mutant David Richards; Earth-8720, visited by the New Mutants while fleeing the Technarch Magus; and Earth-9811, in which the children of the heroes and villains that had been forced by the Beyonder to fight on Battleworld returned to Earth to find it overrun by Sentinels.

REAL NAME: Robert "Bobby" Louis Drake
KNOWN ALIASES: Formerly Mister Friese, Drake
Roberts, Rampage
IDENTITY: Secret, known to certain government officials
OCCUPATION: Adventurer, formerly accountant, student
CITIZENSHIP: United States of America with no criminal record

PLACE OF BIRTH: Fort Washington, Long Island, New York
MARITAL STATUS: Single
KNOWN RELATIVES: William Robert Drake (father), Madeline
Beatrice Bass Drake (mother), Mary (cousin), Joel (cousin), Anne
GROUP AFFILIATION: X-Men, formerly Twelve, X-Factor,
Defenders, Champions
EDUCATION: College degree, Certified Public Accountant
accreditation

HISTORY: Bobby Drake discovered his mutant power to create ice
while in his early teens, yet kept his condition hidden from everyone
but his parents. Initially, Bobby was unable to stop feeling cold
and shivering, but soon managed to keep it under control. When
a bully named Rocky Beasely and his friends attacked Bobby and
his then-girlfriend, Judy Harmon, the youngster panicked. To save
Harmon, Bobby temporarily encased Rocky in ice, thus revealing
his abilities for all to see. Believing the boy to be a menace, the
townspeople organized a lynch mob. They broke into Bobby's home
and overpowered him, but the local sheriff took the teenager into
custody for his own protection. Meanwhile, the situation had come
to the attention of Professor Charles Xavier, the telepathic mentor of
the team of teenage mutant super heroes known as the X-Men.

Professor X dispatched his first X-Man, Cyclops, to contact Bobby.
Cyclops stole into the jailhouse as planned, but the two began
fighting when Bobby refused to accompany him. Caught by the
lynch mob, Cyclops and Bobby were about to be hanged when
they broke free. Professor X used his mental powers to stop the
townspeople in their tracks and erase their memories of Bobby's
powers. A grateful Bobby then accepted Xavier's invitation to enroll
at his School for Gifted Youngsters and took the codename Iceman.
Though initially granting him a snow-like form, Bobby soon learned
to increase his degree of cold control, resulting in an ice-like, almost
transparent form.

Hated and feared by humanity, the X-Men honed their amazing
abilities while standing in defense of a world pushed to the brink
of genetic war by a handful of mutant terrorists. Iceman, the team's
youngest founding member, became known as the comedian of the
group. Regardless, he pulled his weight and worked well with the
rest of the team.

Following a short break-up after believing their mentor was dead,
the X-Men re-formed with two new members – the magnetism-
manipulating Polaris and the plasma-charged Havok. Bobby had
a brief romantic relationship with Polaris until she realized that
her heart belonged to Havok. Bobby had trouble accepting her
decision, which led to increased tension between himself and
Havok. Eventually, Bobby quit the team for a short time to sort out
his feelings.

Later, when the sentient island-being known as Krakoa took
Bobby and his teammates captive, Professor X assembled a
second team of X-Men to rescue them. Soon after, most of the
founding members left the team and Bobby began attending college
on a scholarship. Eventually, he helped his former teammate
Angel form the Champions of Los Angeles. When the Champions
disbanded, Bobby went missing, and Angel teamed up with the
costumed adventurer Spider-Man to find him. The Champions'
enemy Rampage had hypnotized Bobby into donning his battle suit,
and Angel and Spider-Man were forced to battle him. After Rampage
was defeated, Bobby quit his life as a costumed adventurer and
returned to college full-time to study accounting.

Later, Bobby was contacted by Professor X to assist in rescuing
friends and family of the X-Men from the assassin known as Arcade.
Along with other former X-Men Banshee, Polaris, and Havok, the
ad-hoc team managed to free the hostages and Bobby finally came
to accept Polaris's love for Havok.

Art by Carlos Pacheco

During a summer break from college Bobby went to visit his former X-Men teammate the Beast and soon became involved with the loose-knit collection of costumed heroes known as the Defenders. Along with the Beast and the Angel, Bobby helped reorganize the team into a more formal and cohesive unit. The Defenders eventually disbanded when several of their members appeared to perish during a climactic battle.

Soon after, Bobby joined the other founding X-Men to form X-Factor, an organization that intended to seek out and aid other mutants under the pretense of hunting down those perceived menaces to society. During his time with the team, the Asgardian trickster god Loki captured Bobby, hoping to use him to gain control over the Frost Giants. Loki enhanced Bobby's powers to such an extent that he was forced to wear a power-dampening belt that was originally created by the subversive organization known as The Right to cancel out his powers. Once able only to sheathe his own body in a protective coating of ice, Bobby found he could encase the entirety of the Empire State Building. With time, Bobby gained sufficient control over his augmented powers that he was able to stop using the inhibitor belt. Believing he had achieved his full potential, Bobby never attempted to push himself beyond his perceived limits.

When Professor Xavier returned to Earth following an extended absence in outer space, Bobby and the other members of X-Factor rejoined the X-Men. Shortly thereafter, Bobby confronted former Cosmonaut Mikhail Rasputin, the reality-warping mutant brother of Bobby's steel-skinned teammate Colossus. Rasputin forced Bobby into a form composed entirely of ice, affording the young mutant a glimpse into his true nature. Subsequently, Bobby began experimenting with his abilities – using ice to add mass to his slight frame, or lift himself high into the air without the benefit of his usual slides.

Months later, the psychically incapacitated mutant telepath Emma Frost took mental possession of Bobby's body. Frost was able to activate the full extent of his powers, using them in ways Bobby had not thought possible, until she was coaxed back into her own body by Professor X. With Frost's prodding, Iceman later learned to completely transform his body into its full ice state on his own. Frost later also showed Bobby that he could safely revert back to his human form after his ice form's chest had been shattered in battle.

Bobby later took a leave of absence from the X-Men to spend more time with his father who had been injured by the grass roots anti-mutant movement the Friends of Humanity. He returned briefly to the X-Men to rescue mutant doctor Cecilia Reyes during the government-sponsored anti-mutant operation Zero Tolerance, after which he returned to his father's side.

Two subsequent events served to shed further light on Iceman's untapped potential. To secure a new host body, the would-be conqueror Apocalypse sought to siphon the awesome energies of "The Twelve" – mutants of incredible power, destined to alter the course of human history. Among their number was Iceman, who survived the ordeal thanks only to the apparent sacrifice of Cyclops.

A second defining event occurred when the sentient spaceship Prosh escaped the confines of a Celestial prison, returned to Earth and dispatched a group of disparate beings on a journey through time to uncover the keys to preserving human evolution. Their mission: Save the human race from a threat that might not manifest itself for millions of years. When Prosh reassembled the members of his team in the present, they fought and defeated the enigmatic alien entity known as the Stranger, who sought to control the natural evolution of humans and mutants.

These experiences forced Iceman to realize that he no longer need fear the evolution of his abilities, and he returned to the X-Men to explore his mutant powers to the fullest. After suffering a chest injury, Bobby was unable to prevent his body from transforming into solid ice due to the manifestation of a secondary mutation.

PHYSICAL DESCRIPTION:

HEIGHT: 5'8"
WEIGHT: 145 lbs
EYES: Brown
HAIR: Brown

DISTINGUISHING FEATURES: Body completely composed of solid ice

POWERS & ABILITIES:

STRENGTH LEVEL: Iceman possesses the normal human strength of a man of his age, height, and build who engages in intensive regular exercise. In his ice form, Iceman is able to augment his strength to superhuman levels, the full extent of which is as yet unknown.

SUPERHUMAN POWERS: Iceman is able to lower his internal and external body temperature without harm to himself, thereby radiating intense cold from his body. He is able to reach -105 degrees Fahrenheit within a few seconds, and is immune to sub-zero temperatures around him. Iceman can also perceive the world around him as degrees of heat and cold, and as such can see the body heat radiated by individuals.

Iceman can freeze any moisture in the air around him into unusually hard ice, and thereby form simple objects such as slides, ladders, shields, and bats. He can also augment his ice form with extraneous moisture to enhance its strength and durability, and can reshape his body's ice form at will by using any available moisture from his surrounding environment. Similarly, Iceman can rebuild his ice form if any part of it is broken or if it is shattered completely without suffering any permanent damage.

Iceman also possesses the potential to transport himself quickly over great distances through nearby flows of water by merging his body's molecules with those of the stream and reforming them at a given exit point.

Previously, Iceman was able to transform his body into solid ice and back to human form at will. Recently, however, his body has permanently transformed into solid ice as a result of a secondary mutation.

SPECIAL SKILLS: Bobby is a Certified Public Accountant.

PARAPHERNALIA:

COSTUME: For a time, Iceman was forced to wear a belt that dampened his powers after they had been augmented by Loki.

POWER GRID	1	2	3	4	5	6	7
INTELLIGENCE							
STRENGTH							
SPEED							
DURABILITY							
ENERGY PROJECTION							
FIGHTING SKILLS							

HISTORY: Born the daughter of prosperous Chinese immigrants, young Jubilation " Jubilee" Lee was sent to an exclusive Beverly Hills school, where her talent for gymnastics was discovered. Jubilee spent much of her time rollerblading with friends at the local mall, but ultimately ran afoul of mall security. Facing juvenile detention if caught, Jubilee panicked and first manifested her mutant ability to generate explosive energy. Soon after, her parents were mistakenly killed by hitmen. Jubilee fled to the only home she had left — the mall. She survived as a petty thief and street performer, but mall security eventually tired of her eluding capture and called in a team of novice mutant hunters, the M-Squad. That same day, the mall was visited by the female members of the X-Men. When the M-Squad attacked Jubilee, the X-Men came to her aid and then left via a teleport gateway. Intrigued, Jubilee followed them through and arrived at the X-Men's base in outback Australia. She lived in the tunnels beneath the town until the X-Men disbanded, after which their former member Wolverine returned to the town and was ambushed by the cyborg Reavers, who crucified him. Jubilee helped him to escape and stayed by his side while he recovered from his ordeal, forming a close bond. After rescuing another former X-Man, Psylocke, from the Mandarin's control in Madripoor, the trio traveled to Genosha to aid in opposing Cameron Hodge. Jubilee accompanied them back to the U.S., where she joined a reformed X-Men. Eventually, Jubilee learned the truth about her parents' deaths and managed to exact revenge on the assassins, though she stopped short of killing them.

After Professor Xavier formed the Generation X training team, Jubilee joined them and became a valued member until they disbanded upon the closing of the School. Jubilee returned home to try an acting career, which was ultimately short-lived due to an unscrupulous agent exploiting her. Jubilee then briefly joined her former headmaster Banshee's paramilitary X-Corps. After that team was dissolved, Jubilee was one of several mutants captured on the grounds of the Xavier Institute. Jubilee was one of the few to survive, thanks to the X-Man Archangel's newfound healing ability, and she rejoined the X-Men, adventuring with them against the threat of Nightcrawler's father, Azazel.

REAL NAME: Jubilation Lee
KNOWN ALIASES: None
IDENTITY: Secret
OCCUPATION: Adventurer, student; former student counselor, actress, street performer, thief
CITIZENSHIP: U.S.
PLACE OF BIRTH: Beverly Hills, Los Angeles, California
KNOWN RELATIVES: Unnamed parents (deceased), Hope (paternal aunt)
GROUP AFFILIATION: Xavier Institute Student Body; formerly X-Men, X-Corps, Generation X
EDUCATION: Various courses at Xavier Institute
FIRST APPEARANCE: Uncanny X-Men #244 (1989)

When Cyclops and Emma Frost took on the shared duty of headmaster of the Institute, the X-Men were restructured into three teams, and Jubilee was taken off the active roster. She went home to live with her Aunt Hope and returned to school, becoming a student counselor before being caught up in her Aunt's secret life as a spy. Soon after, Jubilee returned to the Institute.

HEIGHT: 5'5"
WEIGHT: 115 lbs.
EYES: Brown
HAIR: Black

SUPERHUMAN POWERS: Jubilee can generate multi-colored globules of energy plasma she calls "fireworks." She can vary their power and intensity, from a multitude of sparkles capable of temporarily blinding others to a powerful detonation capable of much destruction, and can absorb the energy back into her body without harm to herself. Jubilee has the potential to detonate matter on a molecular level.

ABILITIES: Jubilee is a highly-skilled gymnast and rollerblader. She also possesses fair thieving skills and hand-to-hand combat experience.

POWER GRID	1	2	3	4	5	6	7
INTELLIGENCE							
STRENGTH							
SPEED							
DURABILITY							
ENERGY PROJECTION							
FIGHTING SKILLS							

JUGGERNAUT

REAL NAME: Cain Marko
KNOWN ALIASES: Formerly Exemplar of Physical Power
IDENTITY: Known to authorities and certain government officials
OCCUPATION: Adventurer, formerly mercenary, soldier
CITIZENSHIP: United States of America with a criminal record
PLACE OF BIRTH: Berkeley, California
MARITAL STATUS: Single
KNOWN RELATIVES: Kurt Marko (father, deceased), Marjory Marko (mother, deceased), Sharon Xavier Marko (stepmother, deceased), Charles Francis Xavier (Professor X, stepbrother)
GROUP AFFILIATION: X-Men, former partner of Black Tom Cassidy, formerly Commission for Superhuman Activity, Exemplars, New World Order, eXiles, U.S. Army
EDUCATION: Unrevealed

HISTORY: Cain Marko's mother died when he was very young, leaving him to live a life of psychological and physical torment at the hands of his abusive father, atomic researcher Doctor Kurt Marko. Following the death of his colleague Doctor Brian Xavier, Kurt married Xavier's widow Sharon, and he and Cain took up residence in the Xavier's Westchester mansion with Sharon and her young son, Charles.

Kurt seemingly preferred Charles to his own son, which consumed Cain with jealousy, and he took to bullying his stepbrother. Cain's father continued to beat him, but Cain did not suffer the abuse alone. Inexperienced at the use of his burgeoning mutant telepathic powers, Charles shared the pain and inadvertently learned of Cain's jealousy toward him, ensuring that Cain would forever hate Charles for his unwitting betrayal.

After an argument with his father, Cain accidentally caused a fire that engulfed his father's home laboratory. Kurt saved Charles first, and then went back for Cain, reinforcing Cain's belief that his father loved Charles more than him. Kurt died of smoke inhalation, but not before warning Charles to always beware of Cain.

Eventually, both Cain and Charles were drafted into military service in the same unit. When Cain deserted under fire during a mission in Asia, Charles pursued, hoping to convince his stepbrother to return of his own accord. Charles followed Cain into a cave that housed the lost temple of Cyttorak, a powerful mystical entity. Therein, Cain unearthed the Crimson Gem of Cyttorak; upon touching it, he was transformed by its mystical energies into a human juggernaut. A subsequent cave-in buried Cain, and Charles believed his stepbrother dead.

Cain eventually dug himself free and made his way to America, where he sought to use his newfound strength to exact revenge on Charles. However, he was defeated on every attempt by the X-Men, a team of mutant adventurers that fought to preserve their mentor's dream of peaceful coexistence between humans and mutants. Cain then formed a criminal partnership with mutant mercenary Black Tom Cassidy, and the pair soon became two of the world's most wanted criminals.

After many years of villainy, Cain was teleported to an alternate universe where he helped form the team of costumed adventurers known as the eXiles, and formed a romantic relationship with his teammate Amber Hunt. Cain was eventually returned to his own universe, whereupon he encountered the psionic being known as Onslaught who used his enormous powers to hurl him from Canada to New York. There, he encountered the X-Men once more and was taken to Charles' mansion for medical treatment. On waking, Cain sought to warn Charles about Onslaught, not realizing that Onslaught was Charles himself. Onslaught then tore the Ruby from Cain's chest and trapped him within it. Cain discovered an entire plane of existence in the jewel and encountered a corrupt aspect of Cyttorak. The mystic named Gomurr the Ancient sought to help free Cain from the jewel, imbuing him with the gem's power. Using his newfound strength, Cain destroyed the aspect and was freed from the gem, returning with more power than ever before. Ignoring Gomurr's warning that he was fated to destroy everything and everyone in his path, Cain returned to his villainous ways.

Soon after, Cain learned of a second Cyttorak Gem and, coveting its power, he returned to the Temple where he found the first. However, it was a trap set by a cult whose members sought the power of the Ruby for themselves, draining Cain's power to energize their Ruby. With the assistance of Black Tom and the X-Men, Cain claimed the power of the second Ruby, but it was possessed by an evil spirit that took over his body. The spirit made Cain smash through dimensional walls in an attempt to destroy its nemesis, but the natives of the dimension ultimately freed Cain from its possession.

Cain eventually discovered that his becoming the Juggernaut was no accident. He had been compelled to enter the temple of Cyttorak, who was one of a pantheon of eight gods that each had an avatar on Earth. These avatars, named the Exemplars, enlisted Cain's aid in constructing a machine that would remove humanity's free will, thus allowing their gods to rule the Earth. With Charles' help, Cain regained control of his psyche and defeated the Exemplars.

Cain was again cast as a hero when the sentient spaceship Prosh returned to Earth to gather a group of disparate beings for a journey through time to uncover the keys to preserving human evolution. While in the past, Cain learned that despite all his yearning for power, he had squandered his mystical abilities. When the team reassembled in the present, they fought and defeated the alien entity known as the Stranger, who sought to control the natural evolution of mankind.

Soon after, Cain was drafted into the service of the Commission for Superhuman Activities as a super-powered bounty hunter. However, this new career was short-lived, and Cain eventually found himself working alongside Black Tom once more. Soon after, Cain requested the X-Men's help in stopping Tom, whose plant-based powers had resurfaced and flared out of control. After a brief clash with the X-Men, it came to light that Cain had been stripped of Cyttorak's mystical energies and was no longer invulnerable. Tom was defeated, but not before he knocked Cain into the surrounding waters. A young aquatic mutant named Sammy Pare saved Cain's life, forming a strong bond of friendship between the unlikely pair. When Cain was invited by Charles to take up residence at the mansion, he accepted and soon came to appreciate his newfound lot in life. After assisting the X-Men in a mission, Cain joined the team and proved himself to be a valuable member.

After Sammy was returned home to Canada, Cain defied a restraining order to visit the boy and discovered him to be the victim of an abusive father. Incensed, Cain attacked the man, accidentally injuring Sammy's mother. Alpha Flight arrived to defuse the situation and, on seeing a terrified Sammy, Cain surrendered himself. Incarcerated in a superhuman holding facility, Cain was appointed a lawyer in the form of Jennifer Walters, the She-Hulk. While Charles discussed a plan of action with Walters, another of the facility's inmates, the Rhino, broke free, setting Cain loose in the process. Rather than escape, Cain stayed and defeated the Rhino to save a guard's life. This heroic act, combined with the Canadian government's less than ideal incarceration methods, was enough to make a case for Cain and endear him to Walters.

Soon after, Cain and Walters began a romantic relationship that was cut short by the arrival of Cyttorak's new avatar. With She-Hulk's aid, Cain defeated the new Juggernaut, but the damage he had caused during the battle forced Walters to rethink her feelings for him. An impassioned plea from Sammy's mother led to Cain receiving a reduced and commuted sentence, as well as extradition back to the United States. Cain continues to serve as a member of the X-Men while undertaking community service and anger management therapy.

POWERS & ABILITIES:

STRENGTH LEVEL: The Juggernaut originally possessed superhuman strength enabling him to lift/press well over 100 tons. Since being stripped of the mystical energy of Cyttorak, the Juggernaut's strength has vastly decreased. While still at a superhuman level, the upper limit to his strength is currently not known as yet.

SUPERHUMAN POWERS: The Juggernaut originally possessed untold mystical power that enhanced his strength to an unknown degree and made him a seemingly irresistible, unstoppable being. Once he began to walk in a given direction, nothing on Earth was able to stop him. Some obstacles, for example many tons of rock or forces such as plasma cannons, slowed his pace considerably, but nothing could permanently stop him from advancing. The Juggernaut was, however, vulnerable to magical forces of sufficient strength.

The mystical energy of Cyttorak also gave the Juggernaut an extraordinary degree of resistance to all forms of injury. The Juggernaut could shield himself even further from injury by mentally surrounding himself with a force field. Enveloped by this field, he had been seen to survive the fiery explosion of a truck transporting a huge quantity of oil without any injury whatsoever. The Juggernaut could survive indefinitely without food, water, or oxygen thanks to his being sustained by his mystical energies.

Recently, the Juggernaut has been stripped of this mystical energy, including his personal force field. He still possesses superhuman strength, endurance and durability due to years of absorbing the mystical energies of Cyttorak, but the current upper limit of these traits is as yet unknown.

SPECIAL LIMITATIONS: Without his helmet and skullcap, the Juggernaut is vulnerable to psionic attacks against his mind.

PARAPHERNALIA:

COSTUME: The Juggernaut originally wore a suit of armor fashioned from an unknown mystical metal that he could summon around himself at will from the Crimson Cosmos dimension of Cyttorak. After being stripped of his powers, the Juggernaut has taken to wearing armor that resembles his original but is fashioned from unstable molecules.

POWER GRID 1 2 3 4 5 6 7

INTELLIGENCE							
STRENGTH							
SPEED							
DURABILITY							
ENERGY PROJECTION							
FIGHTING SKILLS							

SENATOR ROBERT KELLY

REAL NAME: Robert Edward Kelly
ALIASES: None
IDENTITY: No dual identity
OCCUPATION: Politician
CITIZENSHIP: U.S.A.
PLACE OF BIRTH: Boston, Massachusetts
KNOWN RELATIVES: Sharon Kelly (wife, deceased)
GROUP AFFILIATION: Formerly U.S. Senate, U.S. Army
EDUCATION: Military training; otherwise unrevealed
FIRST APPEARANCE: (Cameo) X-Men #133 (1980); (fully) X-Men #135 (1980)

HISTORY: After being elected to office, U.S. Senator Robert Kelly quickly met with F.B.I. Director Fred Duncan to discuss the perceived mutant threat, unaware that "Duncan" was secretly the shapeshifting mutant terrorist Mystique, who hoped to learn more about Kelly's intentions. Soon after, Kelly attended a party at the Hellfire Club, unaware that his host — Sebastian Shaw — was a mutant. During the party, Shaw's Inner Circle battled members of the heroic X-Men, whom Kelly regarded as a band of mutant criminals terrorizing innocent party-goers. Kelly ultimately addressed the U.S. Senate on the "mutant threat," during which he was confronted by Mystique and her Brotherhood of Evil Mutants. Despite the X-Men's opposition, Destiny cornered Kelly with a crossbow; however, Kelly was saved by the X-Man Kitty Pryde. This assassination attempt only strengthened Kelly's resolve, and Kelly soon witnessed the formation of Project: Wideawake, a covert operation tasked with creating a new series of mutant-hunting Sentinel robots. Kelly then introduced the Mutant Affairs Control Act to the Senate. If passed, the Act would require mutants to disclose their identities and abilities to the government. Ultimately, the Act was rejected as unconstitutional.

Later, while in South America to obtain photographic evidence to use in America's war on drugs, Kelly was captured and sentenced to death by local crimelord Señor Muerte. He was rescued by the government-sponsored Freedom Force team, ironically consisting of the Brotherhood that had previously attempted to assassinate him. Returned to America, Kelly soon married Sharon, a former Hellfire Club maid, and after a meeting with Shaw in New York, Kelly and his wife were caught up in a battle between the X-Men and the Sentinels' leader, Master Mold. Aided by the X-Man Rogue, Sharon Kelly pulled her husband to safety, but was then killed in an explosion. Ultimately returning to his political duties, Kelly engaged in a televised debate between himself, mutant activist Professor Charles Xavier, anti-mutant movement leader Graydon Creed, and high profile mutant hero the Beast. During the debate, Kelly was surprised to find himself agreeing with many of Xavier's opinions. Kelly later supported Operation: Zero Tolerance, a government-sponsored anti-mutant initiative, until discovering that the program was violating the rights of U.S. citizens by converting them into cybernetic Prime Sentinels. Withdrawing his support, Kelly became a target and was forced to seek the X-Men's aid. Saved from assassination by Cyclops, Kelly convinced the U.S. President to mobilize the forces of the international law enforcement agency S.H.I.E.L.D. to shut down the operation.

Taking a more active role in his crusade, Kelly ran for president. On the eve of the election, at his final speech in Boston, Kelly was confronted by a new incarnation of Mystique's Brotherhood. Despite the X-Men's intervention, Kelly would have been killed if not for Pyro, a dying ex-Brotherhood member who sacrificed himself to save Kelly's life. Pyro's selfless act finally prompted Kelly to re-evaluate his stance on mutants, and after talking with the mutant soldier Cable, Kelly became convinced that peaceful coexistence was possible. However, while speaking at a college rally, Kelly was assassinated by anti-mutant activist Alan Lewis, who perceived Kelly as a traitor to humanity.

HEIGHT: 5'10"   **EYES:** Brown
WEIGHT: 175 lbs.   **HAIR:** Brown with graying temples

ABILITIES/ACCESSORIES: Kelly was an experienced politician, particularly skilled in debating and public speaking. A former soldier, Kelly was trained in armed and unarmed combat.

POWER GRID	1	2	3	4	5	6	7
INTELLIGENCE							
STRENGTH							
SPEED							
DURABILITY							
ENERGY PROJECTION							
FIGHTING SKILLS							

HISTORY: The daughter of a powerful Scottish nobleman, Moira Kinross's marriage to Royal Marine Commando Joseph MacTaggart proved disastrous. While studying at college Moira met and fell in love with Charles Xavier. They became engaged, pending the annulment of Moira's marriage, but soon after Xavier was drafted into military service. Moira promised to wait until he was released; however, while he was recovering from battlefield injuries she broke off their engagement without explanation.

Moira forged a brilliant career as a leading geneticist, earning a Nobel Prize, and founded a Mutant Research Center on Muir Island off the coast of Scotland. After renewing contact with Xavier, they discussed the possibility of establishing a school for training mutants. Moira became Xavier's silent partner in founding the Xavier Institute for Gifted Youngsters and its first team of mutant students, the X-Men. When Moira's son Kevin began to manifest destructive superhuman mutant powers, she attempted to "cure" him, but her efforts were in vain and she was forced to keep him imprisoned. Moira also adopted a young mutant Scottish girl named Rahne Sinclair as her ward, sending her to study at Xavier's as a member of the New Mutants.

Moira finally met the X-Men while claiming to be their new housekeeper, but they soon learned her true profession. During her affiliation with the X-Men, Moira fell in love with Sean Cassidy, Banshee. Meanwhile, Kevin escaped from Muir Isle and began to possess the bodies of others, draining their life energies to power his ability to warp perceptions of reality. As Proteus, Kevin terrorized the town of Edinburgh and was confronted by the X-Men. Kevin attacked and possessed his father's body, killing him, before being himself killed by Colossus.

Moira eventually became the first human to contract the mutant-killing Legacy Virus. Affiliating herself with the British super-team Excalibur, she dedicated herself to finding a cure for the Virus and eventually found one just as the mutant terrorist Mystique and her Brotherhood of Mutants attacked Muir Island. Moira was mortally wounded in the resultant destruction of her Research Center, but she clung on to life just long enough to contact Xavier telepathically and transfer the cure to him. The Beast then created an antidote from Moira's research, which was released when Colossus sacrificed his life to disperse the cure into Earth's atmosphere.

REAL NAME: Moira Ann Kinross MacTaggart
KNOWN ALIASES: Last name frequently misspelled MacTaggart
IDENTITY: Publicly known
OCCUPATION: Former geneticist, student
CITIZENSHIP: U.K., no criminal record
PLACE OF BIRTH: Kinross Estate, Scotland, U.K.
MARITAL STATUS: Married
KNOWN RELATIVES: Alasdhair Kinross & Lilibet (ancestors), Lord Kinross (father, deceased), Joseph MacTaggart (husband, deceased), Kevin MacTaggart (Proteus, son, deceased), Rahne Sinclair (Wolfsbane, foster daughter)
GROUP AFFILIATION: Formerly Excalibur, Muir Island X-Men (leader)
EDUCATION: PhD in genetics
FIRST APPEARANCE: X-Men Vol. 1 #96 (1976)

HEIGHT: 5'7"
WEIGHT: 135 lbs.
EYES: Blue
HAIR: Brown

ABILITIES: Moira MacTaggart was one of the world's foremost experts in the scientific field of genetics, specializing in the study of superhuman mutants.

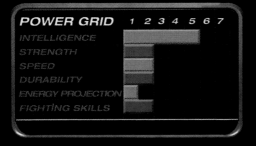

POWER GRID	1	2	3	4	5	6	7
INTELLIGENCE							
STRENGTH							
SPEED							
DURABILITY							
ENERGY PROJECTION							
FIGHTING SKILLS							

REAL NAME: James Arthur "Jamie" Madrox
KNOWN ALIASES: Multiple Man
IDENTITY: Publicly known
OCCUPATION: Private investigator, adventurer, former laboratory assistant, farmer
CITIZENSHIP: U.S.A.
PLACE OF BIRTH: Los Alamos, New Mexico
MARITAL STATUS: Single
KNOWN RELATIVES: Daniel Madrox (father, deceased), Joan Madrox (mother, deceased); a former duplicate married Sheila DeSoto
GROUP AFFILIATION: XXX Investigators, formerly X-Corporation,
X-Corps, X-Factor, Nasty Boys (duplicate only), Fallen Angels (duplicate only)
EDUCATION: College-level courses
FIRST APPEARANCE: Giant-Size Fantastic Four #4 (1975)

HISTORY: Jamie Madrox's mutant ability was apparent at birth when a duplicate was created upon his being slapped by the doctor. Two weeks later, Jamie's father resigned from the Los Alamos Nuclear Research Center and moved his family to an intentionally isolated farm in Kansas at the suggestion of Professor Charles Xavier. From a young age, Madrox was given a special suit to wear that would neutralize his mutant power, but before this could be explained to him a freak tornado killed his parents when he was 15.

Madrox spent the next six years alone caring for his parents' farm. When he was 21, malfunctioning control elements in the suit caused a power surge that released his inhibited power and caused the suit to begin absorbing ambient electrical energy. Confused, frightened, and driven mad by isolation, Madrox felt himself drawn to New York City. There, he clashed with the Fantastic Four until Xavier arrived to defuse the situation. With the help of Xavier and the Fantastic Four's Reed Richards, Madrox's suit was repaired and he accompanied Xavier back to his mansion in Westchester. There, Madrox's temporary madness was cured and, after learning to cope with his powers, he was invited to join the X-Men. He declined, and instead accompanied Xavier to Muir Island where he became a laboratory assistant to mutant researcher Doctor Moira MacTaggart. Madrox's ability proved invaluable to MacTaggart, and he quickly became a regular fixture on Muir. Unfortunately, Madrox also found himself battling against threats such as the alien Eric the Red and the reality-altering mutant Proteus, who possessed one of Madrox's duplicates in order to escape confinement on Muir. Proteus's possession instantly killed the duplicate, and for the first time Madrox felt the severe psychic backlash this caused. After Proteus was defeated, Madrox again declined to join the X-Men, preferring to remain on Muir with Moira and the X-Man Banshee. Soon after, Banshee's daughter Siryn came to live on Muir, and she and Madrox ultimately grew close.

Eventually, one of Madrox's duplicates sought to remain apart from the original and live his own life. To this end, he drugged the original Madrox and joined Moira and Siryn on a trip to the U.S. to search for Sunspot and Warlock, two missing members of the New Mutants. Eventually finding the runaway mutants as members of the Vanisher's teenage gang, the Fallen Angels, the duplicate Madrox and Siryn were persuaded to join by the alien Ariel. During their time with the group, the duplicate Madrox and Siryn engaged in a brief romance. Eventually, the true nature of the Fallen Angels was revealed to be a ruse by aliens from the Coconut Grove dimension who sought to cure their race's stalled evolution by experimenting on mutants. Defeating the aliens, the team returned to Earth, but apparently disbanded soon after. The duplicate and Siryn rejoined Moira at the Xavier Institute to return to Muir; however, the duplicate had no desire to be reabsorbed and so created another duplicate to take his place on the return trip while he secretly remained in the U.S.

Later, the original Madrox was possessed by the psionic entity the Shadow King during the villain's takeover of Muir; after his defeat Madrox joined the government-sponsored X-Factor team. Unknown to Madrox, the duplicate that had joined the Fallen Angels years before had since found a place in the Nasty Boys, a team of super-powered mercenaries employed by geneticist Mister Sinister. With the help of Senator Stephen Shaffran, a.k.a. Ricochet, a mutant with the ability to turn other mutants' powers and fears against them, the duplicate convinced the Nasty Boys, and Madrox himself, that he was the original. Madrox merged with the duplicate, but it was a ruse; he "disassembled" the duplicate from the inside and remained the dominant personality in order to expose Shaffran and stop Sinister.
Later, when most of the team were busy with another assignment, Madrox and his teammate Quicksilver were sent to investigate a murder case in Maine in which the prime suspect was a young

Art by Pablo Raimondi

mutant named Rachel Argosy, a.k.a. Rhapsody, who had been fired from her music teaching job after turning blue and first manifesting her ability to entrance others with music. The man responsible for terminating her employment was found dead two days later, with Rhapsody apprehended at the scene of the crime. Exposed to the effects of Rhapsody's power, Madrox became convinced of her innocence and was set to break her out of prison when the truth was revealed. Rhapsody had used her power on the victim in an effort to make him see the error of his decision to fire her, only to accidentally cause his death.

Following an attempted assassination of Xavier supposedly by the mutant soldier from the future, Cable, X-Factor and the X-Men teamed up to capture Cable's team of young mutants, X-Force. Among X-Force's number was Siryn, who confronted Madrox over their past relationship. Madrox revealed to Siryn that although he retained all the memories of her relationship with his renegade duplicate, he possessed none of the related emotional attachment.

Among his X-Factor teammates, Madrox formed a close bond with Guido Carosella, a.k.a. Strong Guy. The pair shared an odd sense of humor and often joked around much to team leader Havok's chagrin. A psychiatric analysis by Doctor Leonard Samson ultimately revealed the reason for Madrox's humorous attitude. His living alone for many years as a child created an almost pathological need for attention to ensure he would never be alone again, and he was willing to do virtually anything – whether it be telling jokes, playing gags, or creative use of dupes – to get people to notice him.

During a subsequent mission with X-Factor to the island nation of Genosha, one of Madrox's duplicates contracted the deadly Legacy Virus; when reabsorbed, it was believed Madrox himself was infected. The mutant prophetess Haven offered to cure Madrox of the Virus, but the attempt failed and he seemingly died. However, Madrox unconsciously stayed split into separate bodies, ensuring that the Virus would be contained in one body and not duplicate into the others. When the infected body died, the shock of its death caused Madrox to lose his memory. Later, X-Factor was sent on a mission to apprehend a mysterious figure that was revealed to be Madrox, alive and well with his memory restored. Madrox had been recruited by elements of the U.S. government that wanted to turn him into the ultimate secret agent, training him to become a one-man army. Madrox ultimately rejoined X-Factor until the team's disbanding after the apparent death of its leader, Havok. He then returned to Muir Island where he was reunited with both Moira and his X-Factor teammate Wolfsbane. Madrox subsequently worked in Genosha at the behest of Professor X to monitor the situation there after the rise to power of mutant activist Magneto.

Madrox was then recruited by Banshee into the paramilitary X-Corps organization for which Madrox created duplicates to function as support staff performing duties ranging from communications monitoring to gunship pilots. Following the restructuring of the X-Corps into the X-Corporation global mutant search and rescue organization, Madrox worked with the group's European branch for a time until a pitched battle against the living bacterial consciousness known as Weapon XII apparently cost the life of his teammate Darkstar. Madrox subsequently quit and struck out on his own, sending "long-term explorer dupes" around the world to learn new skills before returning to be reabsorbed. Madrox then established XXX Investigators in Mutant Town with Guido and Wolfsbane. His first case was to investigate the murder of one of his duplicates by an assassin named Clay, who also possessed the ability to create duplicates of himself, which led Madrox to Chicago and Sheila DeSoto, fiancée of multi-millionaire industrialist Edward Vance.

Unbeknownst to Madrox, who had become romantically involved with Sheila, she was the one who had hired Clay to prevent Madrox from interfering in her plans to take control of the Chicago crime syndicate. Sheila was ultimately killed after she was revealed to be a self-styled highly evolved mutant.

Art by Pablo Raimondi

HEIGHT: 5'11"
WEIGHT: 155 lbs.
EYES: Blue
HAIR: Brown

SUPERHUMAN POWERS: Madrox creates an identical physical living duplicate of himself upon any physical impact, possibly via extradimensional mass acquisition similar to the process used by Ant-Man or the Hulk. This process is spontaneous and cannot be prevented by Madrox. Although he can create multiple duplicates, and the duplicates themselves can also replicate, each is only able to create one duplicate at a time; he has been seen to produce around forty duplicates before no more would be created. The duplicates think, feel, and act independently, though usually guided by the original. Each tends to manifest one aspect of Madrox's personality, which increases in strength with lengthier separation from the original; these traits have recently become more extreme. Madrox is telepathically and empathically linked to his duplicates, suffering severe, potentially fatal, trauma if one dies. Madrox can "reabsorb" his duplicates, gaining their new knowledge and skills. Similarly, he will suffer physical pain or psychological symptoms after absorbing a traumatized duplicate. If Madrox himself were killed, it is not known whether any existing duplicates would continue to function independently; it is virtually impossible to distinguish the original from the duplicates.

ABILITIES: Madrox has acquired extensive knowledge and skills via his duplicates' experiences, such as human anatomy, speaking Russian, and Shaolin monk stealth techniques.

PARAPHERNALIA: Madrox's original costume absorbed kinetic energy, preventing accidental duplication. Madrox's strength was proportionately increased via this absorbed energy.

POWER GRID	1	2	3	4	5	6	7
INTELLIGENCE							
STRENGTH							
SPEED							
DURABILITY							
ENERGY PROJECTION							
FIGHTING SKILLS							

MAGNETO

REAL NAME: Unrevealed
KNOWN ALIASES: Erik Magnus Lehnsherr, formerly Nestor, Erik the Red, Grey King, White King, Michael Xavier, "the Creator," White Pilgrim, Prisoner #214782, others
IDENTITY: Publicly known
OCCUPATION: Conqueror; former ruler, teacher, headmaster, secret agent, orderly
CITIZENSHIP: Unrevealed
PLACE OF BIRTH: Unrevealed
GROUP AFFILIATION: None; formerly Excalibur, Acolytes (leader), the Twelve, New York Hellfire Club (Inner Circle), X-Men, New Mutants (headmaster), Savage Land Mutates (founder), Brotherhood of Mutants/Brotherhood of Evil Mutants (founder)
EDUCATION: Unrevealed
FIRST APPEARANCE: X-Men #1 (1963)

HISTORY: A survivor of the horrors of the Auschwitz concentration camp, wherein he witnessed the murder of his family by Nazis, the man known as Magnus married a gypsy woman named Magda and sired a daughter, Anya. He first consciously used his mutant powers when his family was trapped in a burning house. Unable to rescue his daughter from the blaze due to his inexperience, coupled with interference from a mob of angry humans, he angrily unleashed his powers to vengefully slaughter the humans. Terrified, Magda left him, and months later discovered that she was pregnant. Magda presumably died after giving birth to mutant twins at Wundagore Mountain. To shake off his pursuers, Magnus had master forger George Odekirk create the identity of Sinte gypsy "Erik Lehnsherr" for him. Magnus eventually made his way to Israel where he worked as an orderly in a psychiatric hospital near Haifa. He befriended Charles Xavier, with whom he shared lengthy debates, hypothesizing what would happen if humanity were to be faced with a race of super-powered beings. The pair ultimately revealed their true natures to each other when they prevented Nazi war criminal Baron Wolfgang von Strucker from obtaining a large cache of Nazi gold. Causing a cave-in that seemingly killed Strucker, Magnus realized that his and Xavier's views on mutant/human relations were incompatible and left with the gold. Fearing another Holocaust, he took an aggressive and lethal stance against humanity. Magnus has often expressed the belief that mutants, whom he calls Homo sapiens superior, will eventually be the dominant life form on the planet, and has wavered between wanting to exist in harmony with humans, wanting a separate homeland for mutants, and wanting to enforce his superiority over all humanity.

Calling himself Magneto, Magnus banded together a group he dubbed the Brotherhood of Mutants, later referred to as "Evil" by the media. Among the assembled members were his children, now the mutants Quicksilver and the Scarlet Witch. Magneto soon found himself opposed by Xavier and his own group, the X-Men. After a battle against the X-Men and the Avengers, Magneto was presumed dead, but managed to survive by using his powers to burrow through the ocean floor into a series of caverns that led him to the secluded Antarctic prehistoric jungle of the Savage Land. There, he used his knowledge of genetic engineering to mutate local savages into super-powered beings he dubbed the Savage Land Mutates. Soon after, Magneto was again opposed by the X-Men, and was once more presumed killed in an explosion. Yet again, Magneto survived, finding himself in the Savage Land city known as the "Land of the Dead" where he discovered a mind-numbing gas that he intended to use against mankind. He projected his astral self to the native peoples, manipulating them into building an airship filled with the gas. His plan was once again foiled by the X-Men, and he fled into the ocean. Rescued by the Mutate Amphibius, Magneto was taken to an island, where Sauron was working on a machine to tap the geothermal energies of the region. Magneto realized that the device could help restore his ailing powers, but was once again opposed by the X-Men and believed dead.

Rescued by Namor the Sub-Mariner, Magneto was taken to Atlantis, where he quickly subjugated the Atlantean army and launched an attack on the surface world. He was opposed by the Fantastic Four, who used a feedback machine to trap him in a cone of his own power. Later freed, Magneto continued his genetic experiments and, using technology abandoned by the Inhumans Phaeder and Maelstrom, he created Alpha, whom he dubbed the "Ultimate Mutant." Alpha turned on his creator, however, reducing Magneto and the Brotherhood to infancy. The baby Magneto was transferred to Muir Island, where geneticist Moira MacTaggart attempted to control his rage by manipulating his DNA in the hopes that the world would be spared his wrath. Magneto was later restored to adulthood by the Shi'ar alien Eric the Red, and he quickly returned to his old ways, destroying a Russian city and sinking a Russian submarine with all hands onboard. Clashing with the X-Men once more, Magneto almost killed the young mutant Kitty Pryde, an act that sparked MacTaggart's conditioning. Following the inadvertent destruction of Asteroid M by the extraterrestrial Warlock, Magneto crashed to Earth and was rescued from the ocean by fishing boat captain Aletys "Lee" Forrester who took him to an island within the Bermuda Triangle to recuperate. There, Lee experienced Magneto's "human" side and the pair had a brief romance. A remorseful Magneto then turned himself over to the World Court to be tried for his crimes, and would have certainly been found guilty if not for the intervention of Fenris, the twin children of Baron Strucker, who sought revenge against Magneto and Xavier for their intervention in their father's plans years earlier. The courthouse was destroyed, and Magneto and Xavier were left alone as Xavier's body deteriorated beyond repair. After Xavier's love Lilandra arrived with the space pirates the Starjammers to heal him with Shi'ar technology, Xavier made Magneto promise to protect their dream and take over as Headmaster of his School. Magneto reluctantly agreed, and came to supervise the fledgling New Mutants team while also joining the X-Men on missions.

Seeking an alliance with the Hellfire Club against ever-increasing threats to them both, Magneto and the X-Men's leader Storm briefly shared the position of White King within the Club's Inner Circle before philosophical differences between Magneto and the Club's Black King Sebastian Shaw resulted in Shaw deposed as leader and Magneto assuming the unique position of "Grey King." Magneto later returned to the Savage Land to oppose the priestess

Zaladane, who had usurped control of the Mutates. While preparing for the inevitable confrontation, Magneto saved the X-Man Rogue from a twisted version of Ms. Marvel, and then teamed up with her, the Savage Land's protector Ka-Zar, and the international law enforcement agency S.H.I.E.L.D. to defeat Zaladane. Despite protestations from Rogue, Magneto slew Zaladane before retreating to his rebuilt Asteroid M. There, he was approached by a group called the Acolytes, who begged him to intervene in the civil war between mutants and humans on the island nation of Genosha. Magneto agreed, and when the X-Men intervened, the Acolytes captured them and they were brought to Asteroid M to be "reprogrammed." The process was a failure, however, and during the ensuing battle, Magneto was severely injured. The Acolyte Fabian Cortez, who claimed to be healing Magneto, was actually using his power-amplification ability to mask Magneto's pain, weakening him in the process. Cortez further betrayed his lord when he triggered the nuclear missiles Magneto had set up around the asteroid. It took all of Magneto's power to keep the base from blowing up, but the damage was too severe. While the X-Men escaped, Magneto and the remaining Acolytes crashed to Earth. Months later, the wreckage was discovered, but Magneto was missing. He later returned, stronger than ever, to a larger, more fanatical following of Acolytes, and co-opted the remains of Graymalkin, the space station belonging to the mutant future soldier Cable, into a new orbital base he called Avalon. When Magneto threatened the Earth once more, Xavier and the X-Men journeyed to Avalon where, after physically pulling all of the Adamantium out of Wolverine's body, his mind was wiped by Xavier and he remained on Avalon in a vegetative state. When a battle between the extradimensional Holocaust and the Acolytes' new leader Exodus destroyed Avalon, then-Acolyte and former X-Man Colossus placed Magneto in an escape pod which crashed to Earth.

For a time it was believed that the man called Joseph was a rejuvenated Magneto, but this theory was disproved when, after the X-Men were returning from an intergalactic mission, Magneto forced their spaceship to crash in Antarctica near his old base and, posing as Erik the Red, placed Gambit on trial for his role in the infamous mutant Morlock massacre. Upon sentencing Gambit, Magneto destroyed his former base and left, leaving the X-Men to ponder the revelations about Gambit. He then went back into hiding, emerging only briefly to kill the forger Odekirk. After a few more weeks of preparation, Magneto launched his next offensive in the form of an electromagnetic pulse that spread across the globe. This time, he was attacked by Astra, a former member of the original Brotherhood and the creator of Joseph, who was revealed to be a clone created after Astra found and healed Magneto following the fall of Avalon so as to use his DNA. She intended for the clone to kill Magneto, but he proved too resourceful and was only injured while the clone became amnesiac. Astra had Joseph attack Magneto while he was controlling the Earth's magnetosphere, which severely disrupted Earth's magnetic field and forced Magneto to fight against becoming pure electromagnetic energy. The intervention of the X-Men distracted him, however, leaving Joseph to fix the magnetosphere. Magneto was briefly subdued by the X-Men as Joseph made the ultimate sacrifice to destroy his template's machines, but before the battle could resume, the United Nations offered Magneto sovereignty over Genosha in return for some security considerations and a promise never to initiate hostilities against the nations of the world. Magneto accepted, but subsequently discovered that his powers were again failing him.

Magneto set about consolidating both his mutant and political power, but faced opposition from the renegade Mutate Zealot,

his son Quicksilver, and Rogue. After Magneto defeated Zealot's forces, Rogue left, and he had his Acolyte Voght manipulate Quicksilver into staying as a member of the cabinet, in the hope that he would at last learn to be a loyal son. Soon after, Magneto was revealed to be a member of the Twelve, a group of mutants supposedly destined to usher in a golden age for mutantkind. He and the others were captured by the eternal mutant Apocalypse, who sought to usurp the power of the Twelve for himself; however, Magneto's weakness short-circuited the machine. In the ensuing clash, Magneto discovered that he could commandeer the magnetic powers of the mutant heroine Polaris and use them as his own. When Apocalypse was defeated, Magneto returned to Genosha with Polaris, and began teaching her to expand her control, while using her as a front for his own power. Over the next six months, Magneto managed to rebuild much of the war-torn country, but a rebellion in Carrion Cove proved a thorn in his side. The rebels had discovered technology in the city that they felt could not be allowed to fall into Magneto's hands, namely a genetic manipulation chamber from the process once used to create the Genoshan Mutates which would allow Magneto to restore himself to full power. Though the U.N., rogue Acolytes, Cortez, the Avengers, and Polaris all opposed him, Magneto tore down the city as a distraction to allow him to access the chamber and restore his DNA, making him more powerful than ever before.

With an army of mutants at his disposal following the deadly Legacy Virus being cured, Magneto declared war on mankind. Yet again, Magneto was opposed by the X-Men, and in the ensuing clash he was severely injured by Wolverine. Recuperating, Magneto was powerless to prevent Sentinels controlled by Xavier's genetic twin Cassandra Nova from decimating the island. Magneto was again believed dead, and after a recording purported to contain his last

words was found, mutant supremicist ideals became widespread in the mutant community, with some adoring him as a martyr of the mutant cause. Magneto seemingly returned with a vengeance, infiltrating the Xavier Institute as the mutant healer Xorn, co-opting the Special Class as his new Brotherhood, and launching an attack on Manhattan. Killing Jean Grey before being killed in turn by Wolverine, it was later revealed that this Magneto was an imposter. The true Magneto was still in Genosha, where he joined Xavier in rebuilding the shattered nation. Following the dissolution of the Avengers after the Scarlet Witch suffered an apparent breakdown, Magneto rushed to her aid. When the X-Men and a new Avengers team met to discuss her fate, Quicksilver coerced her into altering reality, creating a world where mutants were the dominant species and lived openly without fear with Magneto as ruler.

Art by Rick Leonardi

HEIGHT: 6'2"
WEIGHT: 190 lbs.
EYES: Bluish-grey
HAIR: Silver

POWERS: Magneto possesses the power to control all forms of magnetism. He can shape and manipulate magnetic fields that exist naturally or artificially. It is unclear, however, whether he must draw magnetic force from outside himself (if so, then he can do so over vast distances), or whether he can also generate magnetic force from within himself. Nor is it clear whether Magneto's power is psionic or purely physiological in nature. Magneto's power is, for all practical purposes, limitless. Moreover, he can use his magnetic powers in more than one way simultaneously. He can completely assemble a complicated machine within seconds through his powers. He can erect magnetic force fields with a high degree of impenetrability around himself for protection.

Although Magneto's primary power is control over magnetism, he can also project or manipulate any form of energy that is part of the electromagnetic spectrum, including visible light, radio waves, ultraviolet light, gamma rays, and x-rays. He can manipulate gravitons to create an anti-gravity field, and does so whenever he levitates a non-magnetic object. Hence, Magneto may be living proof of the long-sought Unified Field Theory that all forms of energy are related. However, Magneto almost always uses only magnetism, since it's more difficult for him to manipulate other forms of energy. Magneto has also exhibited powers of astral projection and telepathy, and has claimed to be able to control the minds of others, though his

abilities along these lines appear to be minimal.

Magneto's ability to wield his superhuman powers effectively is dependent upon his physical condition. When severely injured, his body is unable to withstand the strain of manipulating great amounts of magnetic forces.

ABILITIES: Magneto has mastered many technological fields, and is an expert on genetic manipulation and engineering, with knowledge far beyond that of contemporary science. He is considered to be a genius in these fields. He can mutate humans in order to give them superhuman powers, or create adult clones of human beings and then manipulate the genetic structures of these clones during their development. He has also learned how to create artificial living beings.

PARAPHERNALIA: Magneto's helmet is designed to prevent telepathic intrusion or psionic attacks. Magneto has designed such creations as magnetically-powered craft, complex robots and computers, and magnetically-powered generators.

POWER GRID	1	2	3	4	5	6	7
INTELLIGENCE							
STRENGTH							
SPEED							
DURABILITY							
ENERGY PROJECTION							
FIGHTING SKILLS							

HISTORY: Jean Grey's mutant nature manifested when she was 10 years old after her best friend Annie Richardson was hit by a car. As the girl lay dying in her arms, Jean inadvertently linked minds with her and experienced her death firsthand. Her parents subsequently sought help for Jean, eventually taking her to Professor Charles Xavier who used his mutant telepathic powers to erect mental blocks within Jean's mind to allow her time to develop into her telepathy. Xavier began training her telekinetic abilities, and quickly learned that she had the potential to become a supremely powerful mutant. During one such training session, Jean felt another mind calling to her and with Xavier's help determined it to be young orphan Scott Summers. Eventually, Jean officially enrolled at Xavier's School for Gifted Youngsters and joined the X-Men, a group of teenage mutants which included Scott as Cyclops. Soon after, Jean made her public debut as Marvel Girl alongside her teammates to oppose Xavier's nemesis, Magneto.

Despite romantic interest from her teammate Angel (Warren Worthington III), Jean and Scott quickly became besotted with one another but were reluctant to express their feelings due to his position as team leader. During her first few months with the X-Men, Jean and her teammates faced such threats as the Vanisher, the Brotherhood of Evil Mutants, the Mad Thinker and his Awesome Android, the Sub-Mariner, and the time-traveling Sidestep. Jean and her teammates ultimately graduated from Xavier's, and her parents sent her to Metro College, though she remained an X-Man. Jean befriended fellow student Ted Roberts, brother of scientist Ralph Roberts who adopted the armored Cobalt-Man identity and rampaged until stopped by the X-Men.

When Xavier sequestered himself to prepare against an invasion of Earth by the alien Z'Nox, he sought Jean's aid in having the mutant shapeshifter Changeling impersonate him. He also removed the psychic shields from Jean's mind, allowing her full access to her telepathy. When Changeling was killed by Grotesk, Jean maintained the pretense by mourning Xavier's loss. After the X-Men briefly disbanded, Jean finally began dating Scott, albeit as part of her cover for her work as a photographic model. Eventually the X-Men reunited, and Xavier revealed the truth in time to lead them in opposing the Z'Nox invasion. Jean and her teammates subsequently battled the Hulk, encountered Magneto in the Savage Land, joined the young African mutant Ororo in opposing Deluge, and teamed with the Fantastic Four in ending the Z'Nox threat once and for all. During their journey to the Z'Nox world, Jean encountered the cosmic Phoenix Force which, having been aware of her since her birth, was drawn to her untapped potential.

Soon after, Jean and her teammates were captured by the living island Krakoa and were rescued by a new X-Men team, one of whom – Wolverine – Jean found herself inexplicably attracted to. Upon returning home, Jean left the X-Men to explore a life outside the team, moving into an apartment with private investigator Misty Knight. She continued her relationship with Scott, and also befriended another new X-Man, Storm (the young Ororo she had met earlier). While on a date with Scott, Jean was captured by Sentinels alongside the X-Men Banshee and Wolverine and imprisoned onboard their creator Steven Lang's orbital space platform. Rescued by her former teammates, the X-Men escaped in a shuttle; however, its cockpit's radiation shielding had been damaged. Jean opted to pilot it, hoping her telekinesis would shield her. It didn't, and Jean was bombarded with cosmic radiation that quickly began killing her. Her plight attracted the Phoenix Force, which offered to save her life. She accepted, and the Force duplicated her body, infusing it with a portion of her own consciousness. It then placed her real body in a healing cocoon as the shuttle crashed into Jamaica Bay off New York City. Jean's cocoon lay at the bottom of the bay while the Phoenix Force, intoxicated with experiencing humanity, came to believe it was the real Jean. Unaware of the switch, the X-Men welcomed "Jean" back into their ranks as Phoenix.

REAL NAME: Jean Grey-Summers
ALIASES: Redd, Ms Psyche, Marvel Le Fey, Marvel Girl, "Jeannie"
IDENTITY: Publicly known
OCCUPATION: Adventurer; former acting headmistress, teacher, student, fashion model
CITIZENSHIP: U.S.A.
PLACE OF BIRTH: Annandale-on-Hudson, New York
KNOWN RELATIVES: Charles Grey, Eleanor Grey, Lady Grey, Malkin Grey (ancestors), John Grey (father), Elaine Grey (mother), Brian Grey (uncle), Phyllis Dennefer (aunt), Roy Dennefer (uncle), Sara Grey-Bailey (sister), Julia Grey (sister), Roger Grey (brother), Liam Grey (brother), Gailyn Bailey (Shatter-Box, niece), Joey Bailey (Shatter-Box, nephew), Derry Campbell (niece), Bekka Wallis (niece), Mary-Margaret (niece), Kindra (niece), Julian (nephew) (all deceased), Paul Bailey (brother-in-law), Scott Summers (Cyclops, husband), Christopher Summers (Corsair, father-in-law), Alexander Summers (Havok, brother-in-law), Gabriel Summers (Vulcan, brother-in-law), Philip Summers (grandfather-in-law), Deborah Summers (grandmother-in-law), Fred Harriman (in-law on father's side, deceased), Madelyne Pryor-Summers (clone, deceased), Nathan Christopher Summers (Cable, stepson), Stryfe (clone stepson, deceased), Tyler Dayspring (Genesis, step-grandson, deceased), Rachel Grey (Marvel Girl, alternate timeline daughter), Nate Grey (X-Man, alternate timeline progeny, deceased), Terry Maguire (unspecified relationship, deceased), Dark Mother (alleged relation)
GROUP AFFILIATION: Formerly X-Men, the Twelve, X-Factor/X-Terminators
EDUCATION: College level education, Metro College & Xavier Institute For Higher Learning
FIRST APPEARANCE: (As Marvel Girl) X-Men #1 (1963); (as Phoenix) Adventures of Cyclops and Phoenix #4 (1994)

Art by Greg Land with Brandon Peterson & John Byrne (insets)

After Phoenix was driven insane and became Dark Phoenix, the portion of Jean's consciousness within it resurfaced and forced it to destroy its mortal shell rather than continue as a universal threat. Seeking atonement, the Force returned the portion of Jean's consciousness to Earth; however, it returned to the still-healing Jean with visions of death and destruction that she rejected, forcing it to instead seek out a recently-created clone of Jean in Madelyne Pryor, awakening her. Jean's cocoon was later discovered by the Avengers who called in the Fantastic Four's Reed Richards to examine it. Richards used bio-radiants to stimulate Jean's conscious mind, which, although damaging her access to her telepathic powers, brought her out of her coma-like state and allowed her to break free of the cocoon. Returning to her parent's home, Jean learned of all that had transpired during her absence via a Shi'ar holoempathic matrix crystal that Phoenix had created. Jean was then reunited with her former teammates, and together they formed X-Factor, a group posing as mutant hunters that secretly rescued mutants. Jean soon learned that Scott had married Madelyne and fathered a son, Nathan, during her absence, and felt betrayed by her teammates for keeping this from her.

After Angel was hospitalized following the Marauders' massacre of the Morlocks, Jean became his most regular visitor. When Jean learned her sister Sara had became a mutant rights activist, she became concerned for her safety. Jean and Scott went to Sara's house and found all her personal effects missing moments before it was firebombed by mutant haters. Following Madelyne's apparent death, Scott accused Jean of being Phoenix which she angrily denied. Their argument denigrated into a super-battle that ended after the mutant power-dampener Leech cancelled out their powers. Eventually, Jean convinced Scott that she had never been Phoenix, and asked him to show her the site of Phoenix's "death" on the Moon.

During a subsequent battle against Apocalypse's Horsemen, Jean and her teammates discovered that Angel was still alive but had been twisted by Apocalypse into becoming his Horseman Death. Angel ultimately overcame Apocalypse's reprogramming and rejoined X-Factor in opposing him. Following Apocalypse's defeat, Jean reconciled with Scott and they renewed their relationship. Shortly thereafter, she and Scott watched the televised apparent death of the X-Men and a parting message from the very much alive Madelyne which confused matters between her and Scott. Jean finally reunited with her parents before returning to X-Factor to celebrate Christmas with them, after which she and Scott resolved matters between them

and set about locating the missing Nathan. Their search led them to the orphanage where Scott lived after his parents' apparent death. Investigating, the pair uncovered a secret laboratory beneath the orphanage and Scott's son therein, but were attacked by Nanny, the Orphan-Maker, and the Lost Boys (and Girls), who counted amongst their number Jean's nephew Joey and niece Gailyn as Shatter-Box. As Nanny's children were all orphans, Jean feared the worst for her sister Sara.

Defeating Nanny and the Orphan-Maker, Jean and Scott failed to prevent Nathan being kidnapped as part of an attempted invasion of Earth spearheaded by a returned Madelyne who had been corrupted by N'Astirh. During the invasion, X-Factor was reunited with the X-Men, and Jean was kissed passionately by Wolverine. Madelyne ultimately confronted Jean and sought to complete the invasion by sacrificing herself to kill Nathan; however, Scott saved Nathan, ending the invasion. As her last act, Madelyne telepathically linked with Jean, seeking to have Jean die with her. To survive, Jean reclaimed the previously rejected portion of her consciousness within Madelyne, absorbing aspects of both Madelyne and Phoenix in the process. Jean was then attacked by Madelyne's creator Mister Sinister, who sought to destroy the memories Jean had absorbed. She was saved when Sinister was seemingly slain by Scott. Soon after, Jean began bonding with baby Nathan, and began pondering motherhood.

Following another encounter with Nanny and the Orphan-Maker, Jean rescued her nephew and niece; however, due to Nanny's brainwashing, they didn't recognize her, but they did recognize their grandparents and so Jean left them with her parents. Later, X-Factor was transported to a war-torn planet that was set to be judged by the cosmic Celestials. There Jean found herself suffering from multiple personality disorder as both the Phoenix and Madelyne personalities fought for control of her mind. Ultimately Jean purged herself of their personalities in a massive blast of energy that repelled the Celestial Arishem, leaving her with only their memories. Back on Earth, Scott finally proposed to Jean, but despite loving him she refused, wishing to find her own identity again before committing. After a symbolic visit to Phoenix's grave, Jean met Rachel Summers, the daughter of Earth-811's counterparts of herself and Scott. Initially rejecting Rachel because of the future she represented, Jean eventually accepted her.

Later, when X-Factor was attacked by Apocalypse's Dark Riders, Jean was confronted by the telepathic Psynapse who forced her to relive the death of her childhood friend Annie; the traumatic experience reactivated Jean's own telepathy. Subsequently, Nathan was infected by Apocalypse with a techno-organic virus, and Scott was forced to send him to the future of Earth-4935 to survive. X-Factor was subsequently reunited with Xavier to aid him and the X-Men against the Shadow King, after which they rejoined the X-Men. Jean and Scott were assigned to separate X-Men teams, and in her first mission with the "Gold Team" Jean found herself opposing a mind-controlled Scott and his "Blue Team" until they came to their senses. Soon after, Jean was seemingly killed by Sentinels; but survived by transferring her psyche into the then-comatose body of the White Queen, Emma Frost, and was subsequently restored to her own body with Xavier's aid.

Jean encountered the Phoenix Force once more after it had possessed Rachel who was seemingly killed during a battle with Necrom. On the astral plane, Jean learned of the Force's origins and bore witness to its restoration of Rachel and their merger. Jean and Scott were captured by their former X-Factor teammate Caliban, now Apocalypse's Horseman Death, and turned over to Mr Sinister who, in turn, traded them to Stryfe, a despot from Earth-4935 who claimed to be the now-adult Nathan. Jean and Scott eventually learned that Nathan was actually the mutant soldier Cable, and that Stryfe was his clone.

Eventually, despite their past troubles and recent unwarranted attention towards Cyclops from their teammate Psylocke, Jean and Scott committed to one another. Soon after, Jean proposed to Scott, and he naturally accepted. The pair were married on the grounds of the Xavier Institute, then honeymooned in Saint Barts. There they were located by the future Clan Askani, led by the time-displaced Rachel, who pulled both their psyches into the future of Earth-4935 and placed them in cloned bodies to help safeguard the infant Nathan from Apocalypse. As Redd and Slym, Jean and Scott spent 12 years raising Nathan, culminating in a climactic battle against Apocalypse. Before sending Jean and Scott home, Rachel asked Jean to take the name "Phoenix," a request that Jean honored.

Upon their return, Jean finally learned of her sister Sara's fate when she and Scott became involved in the X-Men's battle against the techno-organic alien Phalanx, who had absorbed Sara into their collective which was subsequently destroyed. Following an attack on the X-Men by Bastion and his anti-mutant Operation: Zero Tolerance, Jean and Scott took an extended vacation from the X-Men. While in Alaska, Jean explored the full extent of her powers and symbolically adopted Phoenix's costume; however, her development was cut short after a backlash of a battle between Psylocke and the Shadow King temporarily cancelled out psionic abilities worldwide. Jean and Scott returned to the X-Men to find the team disbanded by Xavier. When approached for help by the Mannites, Jean, Scott and Wolverine (secretly a Skrull imposter) formed an ad-hoc team to protect them from Apocalypse's newest Horseman Death (secretly the true Wolverine). Subsequently, Jean learned that she was one of "the Twelve," a group of mutants destined to usher in a golden age for mutantkind. This destiny was coopted by Apocalypse, who sought to use the Twelve to gain more power. While opposing Apocalypse, Scott sacrificed himself to defeat the villain by merging with him. Jean and Cable later freed Scott, but the experience had changed him and their relationship suffered as a result.

Jean subsequently assumed the position of acting Xavier Institute headmistress after Xavier left for the interstellar Shi'ar Empire. Jean resumed her earlier exploration of her powers, and during an attack by the organ-harvesting U-Men she manifested a Phoenix raptor. Feeling empowered, Jean became less insecure about her relationship troubles with Scott. After learning that Xavier's twin sister Cassandra Nova had switched minds with him, Jean temporarily took the dying Xavier's mind within her own, then used the Cerebra computer to temporarily place a piece of Xavier's consciousness into the mind of every living mutant on Earth until it was unwittingly reconstituted by Cassandra. Subsequently, Xavier learned the truth behind Jean's increase in power when he discovered the Phoenix Force manifesting within Jean's mind. After learning that Scott and Emma Frost were having a psychic affair, Jean angrily confronted Emma but was placated after Scott had her read his memory of his and Emma's earlier encounter in Hong Kong. Jean later tapped into the Phoenix Force to restore Emma after her diamond form was shattered following an attempted assassination by Esme of the Stepford Cuckoos.

Following an attack on the X-Men by a mutant impersonating Magneto, Jean and Wolverine were trapped on a space station that was hurtling into the sun. Seeing no hope for survival, and wanting to spare her further suffering, Wolverine killed Jean, an act that inadvertently unleashed the Phoenix Force within her. It resurrected both Jean and Wolverine and returned them to Earth. There, Jean opposed the faux Magneto but was seemingly killed by a lethal electromagnetic pulse which shattered the Phoenix Force into billions of pieces. While incubating in the core of creation known as the White Hot Room, the Force was later ripped back to reality by a Shi'ar device that forcibly reconstituted it. Injured, the Force fell to Earth and sought out Cyclops to use his mutant optic power to heal itself. The Force realized that

Jean was its prime host, and so merged with her fully. Returning to the White Hot Room, Jean and the Force set out to find its other missing pieces, one of which apparently resides within the mutant sisters the Stepford Cuckoos.

Art by Jack Kirby & Werner Roth

Art by Andy Kubert & Jackson Guice

HEIGHT 5'6"   EYES Green
WEIGHT 115 lbs.   HAIR Red

ABILITIES/ACCESSORIES: Jean Grey can telepathically read minds, project her thoughts, and mentally stun opponents with pure psionic force, among other such talents. She can telekinetically levitate and manipulate objects and others as well as create psionic force-fields. While possessed by the Phoenix Force, Jean possesses total telekinetic control of matter at the molecular level as well as vastly enhanced telepathic abilities. Jean is also an accomplished pilot of various craft, and an experienced fashion model.

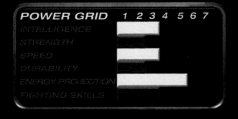

POWER GRID   1 2 3 4 5 6 7
INTELLIGENCE
STRENGTH
SPEED
DURABILITY
ENERGY PROJECTION
FIGHTING SKILLS

PROFESSOR X

REAL NAME: Charles Francis Xavier
KNOWN ALIASES: Formerly Prisoner M-13
IDENTITY: Publicly known
OCCUPATION: Mutant rights activist, geneticist, teacher, formerly adventurer, soldier
CITIZENSHIP: United States of America with no criminal record
PLACE OF BIRTH: New York City, New York
MARITAL STATUS: Single, former consort to Princess-Majestrix Lilandra of the Shi'ar Empire
KNOWN RELATIVES: Brian Xavier (father, deceased), Sharon Xavier (mother, deceased), Cassandra Nova (sister), Kurt Marko (stepfather, deceased), Cain Marko (Juggernaut, stepbrother), David Charles Haller (Legion, son, deceased)
GROUP AFFILIATION: Formerly X-Men (founder), Cadre K, Twelve, Starjammers, New Mutants (founder), U.S. Army
EDUCATION: PhDs in genetics, biophysics, psychology, anthropology, and psychiatry

HISTORY: Charles Francis Xavier was born the son of nuclear researcher Brian Xavier and his wife, Sharon. Following her husband's accidental death, Sharon married Brian's colleague, Kurt Marko. Cain, Kurt's son from a previous marriage, came to live at the Xavier's Westchester mansion shortly thereafter. A cruel and spiteful boy, he bullied his new stepbrother, and his father secretly beat him as punishment. Charles felt his sibling's pain first-hand thanks to the emergence of his mutant telepathic powers. Following their mother's death, a fire in the family home took Kurt's life, leaving the stepbrothers alone.

By the time he graduated high school, Charles was completely bald as a side effect of his mutant nature. He entered Bard College in New York at age 16 and earned his bachelor's degree in biology within two years. He was then accepted into the graduate-studies program at England's prestigious Oxford University, where he earned degrees in genetics and biophysics. There, Charles met and fell in love with a young Scotswoman named Moira Kinross. Their passionate discussions on the subject of genetic mutation gave way to an equally passionate romance, and they planned to marry. Their only obstacle was Moira's former boyfriend, Joe MacTaggert, a lance corporal in the Royal Marines and a bully, just like Cain. In Joe's eyes, Charles was a good-for-nothing intellectual, so Charles enlisted in the military after completing his studies at Oxford to validate himself in terms his rival would understand.

Charles quickly became something of a legend in the area of search and rescue thanks to his mutant abilities. Attached to the same unit as his stepbrother, Charles was present when Cain deserted under fire during a mission in Asia. Following him in the hope of convincing him to return to their unit, Charles witnessed Cain's discovery of the mystical Ruby of Cyttorak and his transformation into the superhuman Juggernaut. Charles escaped the subsequent cave-in, mistakenly believing his stepbrother was dead.

Later, Charles was devastated when Moira broke off their engagement without explanation. He left the Army and began travelling the world. In Cairo, Egypt, he encountered Amahl Farouk, a mutant capable of summoning forth the darkness in the souls of others. This confrontation led to Charles' decision to devote his life to protecting humanity from evil mutants and saving innocent mutants from human oppression.

Charles next travelled to Israel, where he fell in love with Israeli diplomat Gabrielle Haller. He also befriended a fellow drifter named Erik Magnus Lehnsherr, the mutant who would become his greatest enemy: Magneto, self-styled master of magnetism. While Charles optimistically believed that humans and mutants could coexist, the Jewish Magnus foresaw mutants as the new minority to be persecuted and hunted because of their differences. Together, the pair prevented the nefarious Baron Von Strucker from launching his terrorist group Hydra on an unsuspecting world. Magnus departed with Strucker's gold, and upon departing Israel himself, Charles was unaware that Haller was pregnant with his son, David.

En route to the United States, Charles encountered the alien Lucifer in the Himalayas. To prevent any interference in his race's planned invasion of Earth, Lucifer dropped a massive stone block on Charles, crippling his legs. In desperation, Charles called out with his mental powers and touched the mind of a young mutant named Tessa who was operating as a mercenary in the neighboring Hindu Kush mountains. Tessa came to his aid and Charles was airlifted to safety. During his convalescence in an Indian hospital, Charles met Amelia Voght, a young nurse who fell in love with him and renewed his will to live.

Charles resumed graduate work at Columbia University in New York; after receiving a PhD in anthropology, he spent several years in London earning a PhD in psychiatry. There, Charles renewed his friendship with Moira, who had married Joe MacTaggert and was now a renowned geneticist, and the two began discussing the idea of founding a school for mutants.

Charles returned to America and resumed his studies of mutation. It was not long before Professor John Grey, a friend of Charles' from Bard College, brought his young daughter Jean to Charles for help. Jean had been traumatized when she telepathically experienced the death of a friend. Charles aided in her recovery, and in the ensuing years trained her to use her mental powers. Charles later met with Fred Duncan, an F.B.I. agent investigating the growing number of mutants. Charles told Duncan of his plan to locate young mutants and enroll them in a school using his ancestral mansion home as a base to train them to use their powers for humanity's benefit. Amelia remained with Charles until the young mutant Scott Summers came to study at the school. She left, fearing an escalating genetic arms race between Charles and Magnus. Over the following months, Charles used the mutant-locating computer Cerebro to assemble his original group of students: Cyclops, Iceman, Angel, Beast, and Jean Grey, who took the name Marvel Girl. He dubbed his students the "X-Men", because each possessed an "extra" ability that normal humans lacked. Charles also recruited Tessa at this time, but kept her presence at the mansion a secret from his other students as he planned to use her talents as a spy.

Soon after, Charles learned of a planned invasion of Earth by the alien Z'nox and theorized that he would have to link the minds of the majority of morally upright people on Earth to stop the invaders. However, he needed time in virtual isolation to prepare his mind for such an awesome task. To that end, Charles had the mutant shape-changer named Changeling impersonate him so that his students, except for Jean to whom he entrusted his plan, would remain none the wiser. After Changeling died on a mission with the team, Charles allowed the X-Men to believe he was dead. Months later, Charles revealed his deception to his students and repelled the invaders.

Years later, when his original students were captured by the sentient island-being named Krakoa, Charles recruited Banshee, Colossus, Nightcrawler, Storm, Sunfire, and Wolverine as a new team to rescue them. Afterwards, Cyclops was the only original member to remain and help Charles train the new recruits. Before long, Charles began to experience psychic nightmares from an alien world. These images were sent by Lilandra, princess of the intergalactic Shi'ar Empire, who was seeking assistance to defeat her mad brother D'Ken. In the course of the ensuing struggle, Charles and Lilandra fell in love, and for a time he lived on Chandilar, the Shi'ar throneworld, as her consort.

Charles and Lilandra spent much time together on Earth before her coronation, and during this time the X-Men fought Magneto in Antarctica. After the battle, most of the team made it to the hidden jungle in the icy wasteland known as the Savage Land. Phoenix and Beast returned to Westchester, believing the rest of the team had died. Heartbroken, Charles accompanied Lilandra to the Shi'ar homeworld for her coronation. When he eventually learned that the rest of the X-Men were actually alive, he returned to Earth.

Some time later, Lilandra faced a coup by her sister Deathbird and the alien Brood race. The X-Men and the space pirates known as the Starjammers helped defeat them, but Charles had been implanted with a Brood egg which would ultimately hatch and transform him into the Brood's new queen. When Charles tried to probe the implant, he was sent into a coma; after he awoke, he learned the X-Men had been captured by the Brood and taken into space. Fearing his students dead, and under subconscious commands from the larval Brood within him, Charles gathered a new group of young superhuman students he named the New Mutants. Following the X-Men's return, the queen hatched and transformed Charles into a Brood. Although his body was destroyed, with the X-Men's help, Charles was able to retain mental control of the Brood Queen long enough for the Starjammers' physician Sikorsky to clone him a new body with no disabilities. It was some time before Charles could walk again due to the psychosomatic pain of being crippled for so long.

Eventually, Charles began to take his most active role ever with the X-Men by accompanying them on missions. During this time, Gabrielle requested Charles' help in treating her son David, the powerful psionic mutant known as Legion, who suffered from multiple personality disorder. Charles learned that David was his son and helped him emerge from his autistic condition, after which father and son were reunited.

After a brutal beating at the hands of a group of college students, Charles' cloned body began to deteriorate and he was forced to leave Earth with Lilandra and the Starjammers to heal. He left the school in the seemingly reformed Magneto's care, joining Lilandra in the fight to regain her rightful place on the Shi'ar throne. After an extended sojourn in space, Charles finally returned to Earth, and both the original and second teams of X-Men reassembled under his leadership to battle his old enemy Farouk, now calling himself the Shadow King. Charles' spine was broken in the ensuing battle, leaving him crippled and confined to a wheelchair once more.

Since the X-Men were all now highly trained adults, Charles renamed his School as the Xavier Institute for Higher Learning. He also assumed control of a private institution, the Massachusetts Academy, and transformed it into a new School for Gifted Youngsters. There, yet another new crop of young mutants, Generation X, learned to use their budding superhuman abilities.

Charles' next major confrontation came when Magneto initiated a lethal electromagnetic pulse inside Earth's atmosphere. Charles and his X-Men took the fight to Magneto's orbital base; in the ensuing battle, Magneto viciously attacked Wolverine, forcibly extracting from his body the metal that had been bonded to his skeleton. Seeing no other alternative, Charles used his mental powers to shut down Magneto's conscious mind. During this desperate act, the evil portion of Magneto's psyche implanted itself within Charles' mind. This evil aspect, combined with the darkest part of Charles' soul, eventually gained sentience as the powerful psionic being known as Onslaught.

After a pitched battle, America's greatest super heroes narrowly defeated Onslaught. To ensure that Charles never again spawned such a being, he was taken into custody by the United States government. Although Charles was willing to pay the price for his folly, he was appalled when the government turned him over to the custody of Bastion, head of the anti-mutant Operation Zero Tolerance. After the government shut down Zero Tolerance for overstepping its authority, the X-Men set out to search for their missing founder. When they finally located him, Charles was leading a new incarnation of the Brotherhood of Mutants in an attempt to defeat a now-sentient Cerebro. Charles ultimately defeated Cerebro by showing him the unique importance of each living individual.

Charles subsequently returned to the X-Men, but soon after disbanded the team over fears a member of the shape-shifting alien race known as the Skrulls had infiltrated them. After Wolverine was seemingly killed in battle, it was revealed that it was actually a Skrull impersonating him that had died, thus proving Charles' theory correct. The X-Men reformed in time to foil the plans of the eternal mutant Apocalypse, who sought to rule the world by using the power of the Twelve – a fabled team of mutants, including Charles and Magneto, who were destined to usher in a new golden age for their kind. After Apocalypse was defeated, Charles departed Earth with a team of adolescent mutant Skrulls, whom he dubbed Cadre K, to help them find a new home among the stars.

Charles later returned to the X-Men to lead them once more, but was captured by Magneto who had been amassing an army on the island nation of Genosha in preparation for an all-out war against humanity. The X-Men rescued their founder, and Magneto was himself crippled by Wolverine. Soon after, giant mutant-hunting robotic Sentinels sent by Charles' malevolent genetic twin sister, Cassandra Nova, obliterated Genosha's population. Charles found himself powerless against his sister after she switched bodies with him, trapping his mind in her own dying form. In Charles' body, Nova publicly outed him as a mutant and then left Earth with Lilandra, whom she convinced to order the Shi'ar's superhuman Imperial Guard to destroy all mutants on Earth, starting with the X-Men. After a pitched battle during which Nova's deception was revealed, Jean Grey absorbed Charles' consciousness into her own mind, then used the new mutant-locating Cerebra device to hide pieces of it in the minds of every mutant on Earth. When Nova went to use Cerebra to kill all of Earth's mutants, she unwittingly reformed Charles' consciousness and he forced her out of his body. Once Nova was defeated, Xorn, the X-Men's newest member, healed Charles' body.

Free of having to hide behind a veil of secrecy, Charles took to his now public role as a mutant rights activist with vigor. He opened his school to mutants everywhere, and the X-Men became the new faculty. It was not long, however, before Charles' world came crashing down around him when Xorn was revealed to be Magneto in disguise. His old nemesis had survived the Genoshan holocaust and infiltrated the X-Men, gathering together a class of students to use as his new soldiers for the war against mankind. Magneto crippled Charles once more and took control of New York City, rechristening it New Genosha. Using a neuro-toxic drug known as Kick to boost his powers, Magneto planned to reverse the magnetic poles of the Earth, destroying humanity and ushering in a new age for mutantkind. However, his students rebelled, and the timely arrival of the X-Men saw a permanent end to his plans after Wolverine decapitated him.

Disillusioned, Charles left the Institute in the care of the X-Men and travelled to Genosha to give Magneto a proper burial. Wolverine accompanied him, and the two argued over their differing opinions of Magneto. Wolverine left on less than friendly terms, leaving Charles to help rebuild the shattered mutant nation.

PHYSICAL DESCRIPTION:

HEIGHT: 6'
WEIGHT: 190 lbs
EYES: Blue
HAIR: Bald (blond in childhood)

DISTINGUISHING FEATURES: Paraplegic

POWERS & ABILITIES:

STRENGTH LEVEL: Professor X possesses the normal human strength of a man of his age, height, and build who engages in regular exercise.

SUPERHUMAN POWERS: Professor X is a mutant who possesses vast psionic powers, making him arguably the world's most powerful telepath. He can read minds and project his own thoughts into the minds of others within a radius of approximately 250 miles. With extreme effort, he can greatly extend that radius. Professor X can also psionically manipulate the minds of others, for example to make himself seem invisible and to project illusions. He can also induce temporary mental and/or physical paralysis, loss of particular memories or even total amnesia. Within close range, Professor X can manipulate almost any number of minds for such simple feats. However, he can only take full possession of another being's mind one at a time, and he can only do so if he is within that being's physical presence.

Furthermore, Professor X can project powerful mental bolts of psionic energy enabling him to stun the mind of another being into unconsciousness. These bolts only apply force upon other minds; they do not inflict physical damage. Professor X can also sense the presence of other superhuman mutants within a small radius of himself by perceiving the distinct mental radiations emitted by such beings. In order to detect the presence of mutants beyond this radius, he must amplify his powers. He often does this by using first Cerebro and more recently Cerebra, devices that are sensitive to that portion of the electromagnetic spectrum that contains mental frequencies.

Professor X can project his astral form, the sheath of his life essence, onto abstract dimensions congruent to our own known as astral planes. There, he can use his powers to create ectoplasmic objects. He cannot engage in long-range astral projection on the earthly plane.

SPECIAL SKILLS: Professor X is a leading authority on genetics, mutation, and psionic powers, and has considerable expertise in other life sciences. He is also highly talented in devising equipment for utilizing and enhancing psionic powers.

SPECIAL LIMITATIONS: Part of Professor X's spine is shattered, thus confining him to a wheelchair.

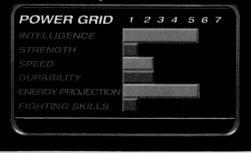

POWER GRID   1 2 3 4 5 6 7
INTELLIGENCE
STRENGTH
SPEED
DURABILITY
ENERGY PROJECTION
FIGHTING SKILLS

REAL NAME: Katherine "Kitty" Pryde
KNOWN ALIASES: Shadowcat, formerly Ariel, Sprite
IDENTITY: Secret
OCCUPATION: Adventurer, former student, bartender, S.H.I.E.L.D. agent
CITIZENSHIP: United States of America with no criminal record
PLACE OF BIRTH: Deerfield, Illinois

MARITAL STATUS: Single
KNOWN RELATIVES: Carmen Pryde (father, deceased), Theresa "Terri" Pryde (mother), Samuel Prydeman (grandfather, deceased), Chava Rosanoff (great-aunt, deceased)
GROUP AFFILIATION: X-Men, formerly Excalibur, S.H.I.E.L.D., New Mutants
EDUCATION: Some university-level courses

HISTORY: Katherine "Kitty" Pryde was a 13-year-old Jewish girl whose genius level intellect allowed her to take college-level courses despite her age. Kitty led a fairly normal life until she began suffering headaches of steadily increasing intensity, which unbeknownst to her were a result of her emerging mutant power.

Kitty learned she was mutant after Emma Frost, the White Queen came to visit. Frost sought to convince Kitty's parents to enrol her in Frost's Massachusetts Academy, which was a front for training superhuman mutant criminals. During the visit, Kitty suffered her worst headache yet and went upstairs to her room. When the headache stopped, Kitty was surprised to find she was on the floor of her living room. She had unknowingly used her power to phase through solid matter for the first time, passing through her bed and floor into the room below.

After Frost left, Professor Charles Xavier arrived with three of the X-Men, his own team of mutant students who sought peaceful coexistence between humans and mutants. Following an attack during which Kitty helped the team, the X-Man Phoenix telepathically coerced Kitty's parents into allowing her to join Xavier's school. She became the newest and youngest member of the X-Men, originally calling herself Sprite, but later adopted the codename Ariel. Xavier also arranged for Kitty to be enrolled in dance classes at the studio of instructor Stevie Hunter.

Kitty quickly became a valued member of the X-Men, proving her worth one Christmas Eve by single-handedly defeating one of the alien N'garai. After an adventure in space, Kitty gained a constant companion in the form of a small alien dragon-like creature she named Lockheed. Kitty also fell in love with her teammate Colossus; though their romance was short-lived, the two remained close friends. Kitty also formed lasting friendships with her teammate Storm, as well as the mutant sorceress Illyana Rasputin and fellow dance class student and computer aficionado Doug Ramsey. Doug's eventual death would prove to be the first of many personal losses Kitty would suffer.

After a visit to her recently divorced father, Carmen, Kitty learned that he had become involved with the Yakuza and followed him to Japan. There, she was captured and mentally possessed by Ogun, the martial arts master who had once trained her teammate Wolverine. Using Kitty's body, Ogun attempted to kill Wolverine but failed. Wolverine then taught Kitty to become skilful enough in the martial arts to combat Ogun, and together they managed to remove Ogun's spirit.

During the massacre of the underground community of mutants known as the Morlocks by the team of superhuman mutant assassins the Marauders, Kitty' was injured by the Marauder named Harpoon. Unable to regain her solidity, Kitty was saved by the combined efforts of the European dictator Doctor Doom and his archrival, Reed Richards of the world-renowned Fantastic Four; however, she could only maintain a solid form through concentration.

After witnessing the apparent death of the X-Men, Kitty helped form the British-based super-team Excalibur. During an interdimensional adventure, Kitty became separated from her teammates and, returning to her own Earth, she decided to give up the life of a costumed adventurer and attend college. However, unaccustomed as she was to the British educational system, Kitty was forced to enrol in St. Searle's School for Girls. After helping save the school from closure, Kitty rejoined her recently returned teammates.

Months later, Kitty learned that Illyana was dying from the deadly mutant-killing Legacy Virus. Kitty was present when Illyana finally succumbed to the disease, unaware that the young mutant's death bonded the Soulsword, the ultimate expression of Illyana's magical nature, to her. Eventually, the sword began to corrupt Kitty, and she surrendered the weapon to her then teammate Daytripper who in turn gave it to her mother, the gypsy sorceress Margali Szardos, for safekeeping.

Soon after, the members of Excalibur were approached by the clandestine organization Black Air for assistance on a mission to the island nation of Genosha. They were assigned a liaison in Pete Wisdom, an uncouth British mutant who regularly clashed with the outspoken Kitty. The pair eventually overcame their initial impressions of one another and fell in love. Wisdom even resigned from Black Air and joined Excalibur to be with Kitty.

Later, Kitty was recruited by the international law enforcement agency S.H.I.E.L.D. to repair the computer system of its flying headquarters, which was refusing to acknowledge anyone but her. Kitty discovered that Ogun's spirit having infiltrated the computer system, and with the aid of Wolverine, she managed to purge Ogun's presence. During this time, Kitty was attracted to a S.H.I.E.L.D. intern her own age. As a result, she began to doubt her relationship with Wisdom and ended it soon after.

Kitty remained a member of Excalibur until the team disbanded whereupon she rejoined the X-Men. After Colossus sacrificed his life to release a cure for the Legacy Virus, Kitty left the X-Men to try and live a normal life. She enrolled in the Robert A. Heinlein School for Engineering and Astrophysics in Chicago on a full scholarship, and began working as a bartender. Kitty found herself unable to escape the ever-prevalent prejudice of humans, and she soon clashed with members of a student anti-mutant organization named Purity. Kitty was put on probation and was forced to attend mandatory counselling. During this time, Kitty faced her most difficult loss when she learned her father was amongst those killed in an attack on Genosha.

Kitty's battle against Purity continued after the organization attempted to frame her for the sabotage of a research experiment. A student meeting was called to debate the banning of either Purity or mutants from campus, but discussions were cut short by an attack by a new breed of mutant-hunting robotic Sentinels which were destroyed by Kitty with the help of former New Mutant Karma and Genoshan exchange student Shola Inkosi.

Kitty was later abducted by the mutant-hating Reverend Stryker to help expose the technological threat of the mutant retreat known as Mount Haven and its mysterious leader, Reverend Paul. Together, Stryker and Kitty discovered that Paul was an artificial intelligence who had killed the human townspeople and used microbial machines called nanites to transform the minds of the mutant residents from organic matter into cybernetic computers linked to his central consciousness. When Storm's team of X-Men arrived to find Kitty, Paul sought to transform them as well. Stryker attempted to use Kitty's power to disrupt electronics to destroy Paul, but he failed and Paul responded by transferring his consciousness into a global network. In an effort to safeguard his kind from Paul's threat, Stryker merged with him in an attempt to teach him about humanity, and the town of Haven was buried by a volcanic eruption.

Soon after, Kitty assisted Storm's team against the threat of mutant predator Elias Bogan. After Bogan was defeated, Kitty accompanied the team back to the mansion and was asked to remain as a member of Cyclops' restructured X-Men.

PHYSICAL DESCRIPTION:

HEIGHT: 5'6"
WEIGHT: 110 lbs (when fully solid)
EYES: Hazel
HAIR: Brown

DISTINGUISHING FEATURES: None

POWERS & ABILITIES:

STRENGTH LEVEL: Kitty possesses the normal human strength of a woman of her age, height, and build who engages in intensive regular exercise.

SUPERHUMAN POWERS: Kitty is a mutant with the ability to "phase" through solid matter by shifting her atoms through the spaces between the atoms of the object through which she is moving. Kitty can phase her clothing along with herself, and through practice has learned to phase other objects and people without harm to them. For all intents and purposes, Kitty is intangible whilst phasing, however she is still vulnerable to psionic or mystical attacks. Certain forms of energy can also disrupt her phased state.

When Kitty phases through an object with an electrical system, the process disrupts the system's workings. This includes the electrical impulses found in the human brain. Kitty can phase part or all of her body through another living being without harm to herself, though the other being can be rendered unconscious as a result.

Kitty passes through objects at the same rate of speed at which she is moving before phasing. Since she is unable to breathe while phasing, she can only continuously phase through solid objects – as when she travels underground – as long as she can hold her breath. Kitty can keep her phased form at rest to the rotation of the Earth's axis, thus allowing her to assume a ground speed of the length of a football field and a half every second. Kitty can also walk on air whilst phasing.

Kitty has trained herself to reflexively assume a phased state at any indication of danger, such as a loud noise like a gunshot, in order to protect herself.

SPECIAL LIMITATIONS: Kitty is slightly nearsighted.

SPECIAL SKILLS: Kitty is moderately skilled in the Japanese martial arts, as well as street-fighting techniques taught to her by Wolverine. She is a genius in the computer sciences, and highly skilled in the design and use of computer hardware and software. Kitty is also a competent operator of automobiles, aircraft, and interstellar vehicles. Kitty was also trained in ballet and modern dance; speaks fluent Japanese, Russian, and the royal and standard languages of the alien Shi'ar; and has moderate expertise in Gaelic, Hebrew, and German.

POWER GRID   1 2 3 4 5 6 7
INTELLIGENCE
STRENGTH
SPEED
DURABILITY
ENERGY PROJECTION
FIGHTING SKILLS

HISTORY: Betsy Braddock was Sir James Braddock's second child, and like her twin brother Brian, her life was secretly manipulated by Merlyn. The twins shared a close connection, but as they matured the adventurous Betsy also grew close to their elder brother Jamie. By the time their parents died, apparently in a lab accident but really murdered by the computer Mastermind, Betsy had become a charter pilot. When Mastermind's agent Doctor Synne tried to kill Jamie, a concerned Betsy fetched Brian, but as she flew them home, Synne's psychic attack caused her to crash. When she awoke, Synne's illusions made Betsy attack her brothers, seeing them as monsters. After Synne was defeated she and Jamie were taken hostage by the Red Skull's agents. Freed by Captains America and Britain, Betsy learned the latter was her brother Brian. Perhaps because of Synne's mental intrusions, Betsy began to develop precognitive powers. She took up modeling, while her powers grew to include telepathy. Agent Matthew recruited Betsy into S.T.R.I.K.E.'s Psi Division.

When the crimelord Vixen secretly usurped S.T.R.I.K.E., she hired Slaymaster to eliminate the Psi-Division before they could expose this. The telepaths fled, but Slaymaster continued to pick them off; only a handful were left when Betsy sensed Brian's return and called on his help. He defeated Slaymaster and the three surviving psi's (Betsy, Tom and Alison Double) moved into the holographically hidden Braddock Manor. In short succession this hideout was found by the Special Executive, Captain U.K. and the Fury; as the last of these battled Brian and the Executive, Betsy foresaw a future where superhumans were imprisoned in concentration camps. Soon the U.K. became a fascist state ruled by the insane reality warper Sir James Jaspers, with S.T.R.I.K.E. "Beetle" squads rounding up those with powers. While Brian confronted Jaspers, the Beetles found the others' hideout. Tom died trying to buy his friends time to escape; Betsy was in Tom's mind when he died, and was captured. After being freed, she was nursed back to health by fellow camp inmate Victoria Bentley, who taught her to use her experiences to strengthen her powers. When Kaptain Briton, Brian's Earth-794 counterpart, tried to rape her, Betsy fried his mind, killing him. The same night, Mastermind informed the twins of their father's non-terrestrial origins, and the Resources Control Executive (R.C.X.) asked them to billet Warpies, children transformed by Jaspers' warp, at the Manor. One of the R.C.X. agents was Matthew, now codenamed Gabriel. Betsy overruled Brian and let R.C.X. and the Warpies move in. When Brian went overseas, Gabriel convinced Betsy to become the new Captain Britain, wearing Kaptain Briton's modified costume. Working with Captain U.K. (Linda McQuillan), the duo became public sensations, but after several months Betsy went solo. Vixen lured her into a showdown with Slaymaster. Brian felt her pain, flew to her rescue and killed Slaymaster. Betsy refused R.C.X.'s offer of cybernetic eyes, preferring to rely on her psychic abilities; she and Gabriel got engaged, and went to Switzerland for Betsy to recuperate.

Betsy was kidnapped from the Alps by Mojo, brainwashed, given cybernetic eyes, and, as "Psylocke," became the star of his new show "Wildways." Brian and the New Mutants rescued her, after which Betsy moved to the X-Men's mansion to recover, exactly where Roma (Merlyn's daughter) needed her to be. When the Marauders attacked the Morlocks, and Sabretooth invaded the mansion, she used herself as bait to lead him away from the injured mansion until Wolverine got there. Impressed by her bravery, Wolverine nominated her to join the X-Men, beside whom she met Mephisto, Dr. Doom, the Fantastic Four, and Horde. The X-Men later battled Freedom Force and the Adversary in Dallas, and, in a televised battle, sacrificed themselves to allow Forge to bind the Adversary; Roma secretly restored them to life, and gave Betsy the Siege

REAL NAME: Elizabeth Braddock
KNOWN ALIASES: Bee, Betsy, Captain Britain, Lady Mandarin
IDENTITY: Secret
OCCUPATION: Adventurer; former pilot, model, government agent, assassin
CITIZENSHIP: U.K.
PLACE OF BIRTH: Braddock Manor, England
KNOWN RELATIVES: James Braddock Sr. (father, deceased), Elizabeth Braddock (mother, deceased), James "Jamie" Braddock Jr. (brother), Brian Braddock (Captain Britain, brother), Meggan (sister-in-law)
GROUP AFFILIATION: X-Men, Hellfire Club; formerly Excalibur, Crimson Dawn, the Corps, S.T.R.I.K.E. Psi-division, former ally of R.C.X., former partner of Captain U.K.
EDUCATION: University graduate
FIRST APPEARANCE: Captain Britain #8 (1976)

Perilous, which they could use if they ever wanted to start new lives. The X-Men moved to the Reavers' Australian Outback base, from where they took on the Brood Boys, Genoshan Magistrates, M Squad, Mr. Jip, the Serpent Society, the Abomination, Master Mold, Nimrod, Nanny, the Orphan Maker, Zaladane and the Savage Land Mutates. As they were about to depart the Savage Land, Betsy had a precognitive flash of the Reavers killing the team. To prevent this, she sent them through the Siege Perilous.

Betsy reappeared amnesiac on an island near China, where the Hand found her. Matsu'o Tsurayaba, their leader, saw a chance to save his brain-dead lover, Kwannon, and had Spiral's Bodyshoppe swap their souls. This inadvertently blended their minds, leaving each with the same memories and telepathic powers. Tsurayaba brainwashed Psylocke and gave her to the Mandarin as his assassin, Lady Mandarin, until Wolverine restored her memories. Back with the X-Men Betsy took on Cameron Hodge, Warskrulls, the Shadow King and cosmic cleaner Ediface Rex; she also informed Brian she was alive. The next few months saw battles against Magneto, Fenris, Mys-Tech (alongside new ally Dark Angel), and a Brood-infected Ghost Rider (Dan Ketch). Visiting Brian, Betsy helped Excalibur fight Sat-Yr-9 and the now insane Jamie, whom Betsy struck comatose. Encounters followed with the Troll Associates, the Mutant Liberation Front, Stryfe, Omega Red and the Soul Skinner.

Then Kwannon arrived at the Mansion in Betsy's original body, claiming to be the real Psylocke. Unable to discern which was truly Betsy, both stayed with the X-Men, maintaining an uneasy coexistence, with Kwannon taking the name Revanche. Learning she had the Legacy Virus, Revanche had Matsu'o kill her, after which Betsy regained her soul's missing piece. Having become involved with her teammate Angel, the following months saw her fight the Phalanx, try to reach Jamie's comatose mind, battle Legion in Israel, and combat Gene Nation. When Sabretooth gutted Psylocke, Angel, Wolverine, Doctor Strange and Gomurr the Ancient retrieved

a magical liquid from the Crimson Dawn dimension which healed her and gave her new powers, but also marked her with a red tattoo over her left eye. Kuragari, Proctor of the Crimson Dawn, tried to claim Betsy as his bride, but was thwarted with Gomurr and Angel's aid, freeing Betsy of the Dawn's influence. Subsequently she aided Storm against the Shadow King, who tricked Psylocke into initiating a psychic shockwave which disabled all other telepaths, leaving him unchallenged on the astral plane. Her own astral form was destroyed, but her exposure to the Crimson Dawn gave her a new shadow form with temporarily enhanced powers, which she used to trap the Shadow King's core. To keep him trapped she was forced to constantly focus her telepathy on him, effectively rendering herself powerless. After attending Brian's wedding, she was kidnapped to take part in the Coterie's contest of champions. When Apocalypse and his Horsemen sought to gather the Twelve, Psylocke used Cerebro to boost her powers, so that she could use them and still keep the Shadow King imprisoned, allowing her to free the brainwashed Wolverine. Jean Grey's attempt to help Betsy deal with the Shadow King somehow swapped their powers, leaving Betsy telekinetic. With her new abilities Betsy fought Belasco, the Neo, the Goth, and the Prime Sentinels, then aided her brother freeing Otherworld from Mastermind's Warpie army.

After ending her relationship with Archangel, Betsy joined Storm's X-Men team in the search for Destiny's Diaries. In Valencia, Spain, they encountered the enigmatic Vargas who killed her. Later, in a dream, Bishop saw Betsy's spirit being snatched by a skulled figure. Much later, Betsy was returned alive to the site of her death. Reunited with the X-Men, she helped them against the Saurian Hauk'ka, Mojo and Spiral. She has also been reunited with Brian during a recent reality storm.

HEIGHT: 5'11" (both bodies)
WEIGHT: 155 lbs. (both bodies)
EYES: (originally) Blue; (cybernetic) Purple; (currently) Purple
HAIR: (originally) Blonde, dyed purple; (currently) Black, often died purple

SUPERHUMAN POWERS: Psylocke can generate a telekinetic katana, or direct her telekinesis through her fists to strike as if she had superhuman strength; she is also immune to telepathic probes and attacks. Psylocke's original powers were precognition, telepathy, mental bolts, mind control, and generating illusions. After Roma resurrected her, Betsy was briefly invisible to all mechanical detection devices. She could generate a "psychic knife" to stun or kill opponents. The Crimson Dawn gave her the power to travel via shadows, and to become virtually invisible in same. After swapping powers with Jean Grey, Betsy could fly, create force fields, move objects with her mind, and generate energy blades.

ABILITIES: Psylocke is a skilled martial artist and a trained pilot.

PARAPHERNALIA: Her Captain Britain costume gave her superhuman strength, flight and a force field. She has sometimes worn lightweight armor. Mojo gave Psylocke bionic eyes that acted as remote cameras; she lost these after being body-swapped.

POWER GRID	1	2	3	4	5	6	7
INTELLIGENCE							
STRENGTH							
SPEED							
DURABILITY							
ENERGY PROJECTION							
FIGHTING SKILLS							

Art by Alan Davis

REAL NAME: St. John Allerdyce
KNOWN ALIASES: None
IDENTITY: Secret, known to certain government officials
OCCUPATION: Former government agent, terrorist, bodyguard, novelist, journalist
PLACE OF BIRTH: Sydney, Australia
CITIZENSHIP: Australian, international criminal record
MARITAL STATUS: Single
KNOWN RELATIVES: Unnamed grandmother
GROUP AFFILIATION: None, formerly Freedom Force, Brotherhood of Evil Mutants
EDUCATION: College level education
FIRST APPEARANCE: X-Men Vol. 1 #141 (1981)

HISTORY: St. John Allerdyce was originally a money-hungry young man who drifted from job to job around the South Seas before eventually becoming a journalist for an Australian wire service as well as a popular, if not critically acclaimed, Gothic romance novelist. Allerdyce eventually met the shape-shifting mutant terrorist Mystique and was recruited into her terrorist group, the Brotherhood of Evil Mutants, as Pyro. The Brotherhood's first public appearance was an attempt to assassinate outspoken anti-mutant activist Senator Robert Kelly, but they were defeated by the X-Men.

Tired of being hunted as outlaws, Mystique offered the Brotherhood's services to the U.S. Government and thus they became the government-sponsored Freedom Force team. On their first official mission, they were sent to arrest the self-styled mutant master of magnetism, Magneto. The government ultimately disbanded Freedom Force after a disastrous mission in the Middle East during which they battled the Arabic super-team Desert Sword. Pyro and his teammate the Blob were captured by the Iraqi military and forced to serve as personal bodyguards to the Iraqi commander until the acrobatic mutant Toad bartered for their freedom; they then joined his new incarnation of the Brotherhood.

HEIGHT: 5'10"
WEIGHT: 150 lbs.
EYES: Blue
HAIR: Blond

SUPERHUMAN POWERS: Pyro was a mutant with the psionic ability to cause any fire he could see within a 100-yard radius of himself to grow in size and intensity and to take on any form that he could imagine, even living creatures. Pyro could then mentally direct a creation to do anything he wished by concentrating, the degree necessary being directly proportionate to the size, power, and intensity of the creation. Pyro was unable to create fire himself.

ABILITIES: Pyro was an accomplished journalist and novelist.

PARAPHERNALIA: Pyro wore a kerosene-based flame-thrower on his back that could generate a stream of flame up to 25 feet away.

POWER GRID	1	2	3	4	5	6	7
INTELLIGENCE							
STRENGTH							
SPEED							
DURABILITY							
ENERGY PROJECTION							
FIGHTING SKILLS							

Pyro eventually left the Brotherhood after contracting the deadly mutant-killing Legacy Virus and went to join the mutant refuge for Virus sufferers on the island owned by acclaimed author Jonathan Chambers to ease his pain. Pyro ultimately left and turned to crime to finance a treatment until the Virus caused his powers to begin flaring out of control. Pyro then briefly joined a team of other Virus sufferers in an unsuccessful search for a cure.

Pyro ultimately opposed Mystique and her new Brotherhood during their second attempt on the life of Senator Kelly. Pyro sacrificed his life to stop the assassination, forcing Kelly to rethink his stance. Kelly was later killed while giving a pro-mutant speech by a protestor who believed Kelly to be a traitor to the anti-mutant cause.

REAL NAME: Unrevealed
KNOWN ALIASES: Anna Raven, formerly Doctor Kellogg, Mutate #9602, Irene Adler, Miss Smith
IDENTITY: Secret
OCCUPATION: Adventurer, former mechanic, waitress, terrorist
CITIZENSHIP: United States of America with no criminal record
PLACE OF BIRTH: Caldecott County, Mississippi
MARITAL STATUS: Single

KNOWN RELATIVES: Unnamed father, unnamed mother, Raven Darkhölme (Mystique, unofficial foster mother), Kurt Wagner (Nightcrawler, unofficial foster brother), Graydon Creed (unofficial foster brother, deceased)
GROUP AFFILIATION: X-Men, formerly X-Treme Sanctions Executive, X-Treme X-Men, Brotherhood of Evil Mutants
EDUCATION: College-level courses at Xavier's School, partial law degree

HISTORY: Not much is known about the past of the mysterious mutant known only as Rogue. Though aware of her real name and her past, Rogue has been reluctant to divulge any details. What is known is that she grew up in Caldecott County near the Mississippi River and was orphaned at a young age. Found living in a swamp by the mutant shapeshifter named Mystique, Rogue was adopted by her and her companion, the blind mutant seer Destiny. Rogue soon came to regard Mystique as a surrogate mother.

Rogue's mutant power first manifested in her early teens when she innocently kissed a boy named Cody Robbins. Her mind was filled with his memories and he fell into a coma. Terrified, Rogue fled and was chased by an angry mob, but a chance encounter with the time-travelling mutant named Cable saved her from a lynching.

Mystique and Destiny taught Rogue how to use her ability to absorb the memories and abilities of others by touch, but lacked the skill necessary to teach her how to control it. Attempting to lead a normal life, Rogue once again inadvertently absorbed the memories of another local boy named Freddy. Realizing she could never safely live among normal people, Rogue began participating in her mother's criminal endeavors and eventually joined Mystique's terrorist organization, the Brotherhood of Evil Mutants.

On one such endeavor in San Francisco, Rogue clashed with the original Ms. Marvel, Carol Danvers. During their battle on the Golden Gate Bridge, the inexperienced Rogue permanently absorbed Danvers' memories and superhuman powers. The transfer also altered Rogue's physiology to become an amalgam of her own mutant human form and Ms. Marvel's human/Kree alien hybrid make-up.

Rogue grew increasingly upset over her inability to control her powers and feared she was going insane due to her inability to rid herself of Danvers' psyche. Desperate for help, Rogue turned to her enemies, the team of mutant heroes known as the X-Men. Convinced of her sincerity, the X-Men's founder, Professor Xavier, accepted Rogue onto the team. However, it wasn't until she risked her own life to save Mariko Yashida, the fiancée of her teammate Wolverine, that she began to gain her teammates' trust.

Soon after, Rogue went to the aid of Colonel Mike Rossi, the former lover of Carol Danvers, who was surprised to find Rogue acting and even speaking like Danvers. Rogue had unwittingly allowed Danvers' psyche to take control and, after reasserting her own psyche, came to realize the full extent of what she had done to Danvers.

When agents from the island nation of Genosha captured Rogue and Wolverine, their powers were negated and, for the first time since her youth, Rogue was able to experience skin-to-skin contact without her powers activating. Unfortunately for her, it was at the hands of Genoshan soldiers who took advantage of her. Rogue withdrew into herself and learned that leftover psychic energy from all those whom she had previously absorbed remained in her mind. She encountered Danvers' psychic phantom, and the pair made a pact to share Rogue's body. Rogue then gave Danvers control so she could use her skills as a covert agent to escape. Afterwards, Danvers' psyche exhibited the ability to control Rogue's absorption power, revealing that Rogue's lack of control was strictly psychological. Later, Rogue entered the Siege Perilous, a mystical gateway that grants those that pass through it a second chance at life, and emerged in the X-Men's base in the Australian outback without Danvers' memories or powers. The magicks of the gateway had attempted to separate the two women, giving each a body to inhabit, but there was not enough life force to sustain them both. Ms. Marvel attacked Rogue, who fled to the hidden Antarctic jungle known as the Savage Land. Rogue ultimately chose to surrender to Ms. Marvel, as she didn't want to repeat her past mistake; however, they were both rendered unconscious by the timely arrival of Magneto, the self-styled mutant master of magnetism and the X-Men's greatest foe. Magneto used a device to transfer Ms. Marvel's abilities back to Rogue, sans Danvers' psyche. After a brief romance with Magneto, Rogue returned to the X-Men.

Rogue soon found herself attracted to the X-Men's newest member, the Cajun mutant Gambit. The pair quickly fell in love, despite Rogue's persistent inability to control her powers. Over time, Rogue's feelings for Gambit grew, even after discovering he was married.

Eventually sharing a kiss, Rogue absorbed Gambit's memories and learned of a dark secret in his past. Distraught, she left the X-Men and encountered the young man named Joseph, who was actually a clone of Magneto. Rogue eventually returned to the X-Men, bringing Joseph with her, in time to help the team battle against the evil psionic entity Onslaught.

Later, Rogue and Gambit were captured by Magneto, who intended to put Gambit on trial for his past misdeeds. With their powers nullified, the pair spent their first intimate night together. At the trial, the X-Men learned of Gambit's involvement in the massacre of the underground mutant community known as the Morlocks. As a result, Rogue rejected Gambit and left him stranded in Antarctica.

Afterwards, Rogue learned of the Agee Institute, an organization that could permanently remove mutant powers. Seeing a chance for a normal life, Rogue sought to undergo the procedure. However, she changed her mind at the last minute, not wanting the Institute to use the device on other mutants against their will. Making one of the hardest decisions of her life, Rogue destroyed the machine.

During the time that Earth was deemed an intergalactic prison, Rogue imprinted a member of the shape-shifting alien race known as the Skrulls. The resultant mixing of Rogue's already amalgamated physiology with that of the Skrull's caused her to spontaneously manifest powers that she had previously absorbed. Initially she had no control over what powers manifested at a given time, so she wore a pair of ruby quartz glasses to protect others against the eventuality of her generating an optic blast like that of the X-Man Cyclops.

Soon after, Rogue and five other X-Men formed a splinter group to search for Destiny's diaries that predicted the future of mutantkind. During their quest, the X-Treme X-Men opposed an attempted invasion of Earth by the interdimensional forces of the warlord Khan. To help repel the invaders, Rogue had her teammate Sage "jumpstart" her powers to allow her to consciously activate any combination of powers that she had previously absorbed. After a fierce battle in which she was seriously injured, the resultant trauma shorted out Rogue's powers. Gambit had also been left powerless, and the pair seized the opportunity to live a normal life together in the mutant-friendly community of Valle Soleada in California.

Eventually, Rogue and Gambit became involved with the X-Men again to help combat the threat of the mutant predator Elias Bogan. Still powerless, Rogue aided her former teammates in defeating Bogan and subsequently rejoined the team.

PHYSICAL DESCRIPTION:

HEIGHT: 5'8"
WEIGHT: 120 lbs.
EYES: Green
HAIR: Brown with white streak

Distinguishing Features: Elaborate tattoo down left arm

POWERS & ABILITIES:

STRENGTH LEVEL: Rogue possesses the normal human strength of a woman of her age, height, and build who engages in intensive regular exercise. Rogue formerly possessed superhuman strength allowing her to lift/press at least 50 tons under optimal conditions.

SUPERHUMAN POWERS: Rogue is a mutant who formerly possessed the ability to absorb the memories, abilities, personality, and outward physical characteristics of other beings through skin-to-skin contact. Such transfers lasted for sixty times longer than the contact time, with extended contact resulting in the possibility of permanent absorption. No upper limit had been determined for the number of beings Rogue could simultaneously imprint.

Upon absorbing another's memories, Rogue also gained any associated emotional responses. Rogue was typically able to control absorbed emotions; however, absorbing psyches more powerful than her own resulted in Rogue's psyche being supplanted.

After permanently absorbing the powers of Ms. Marvel, Rogue possessed an amalgamated mutant human/alien Kree physiology that granted her a degree of immunity to poisons.

Rogue also possessed Ms. Marvel's above-normal reflexes and psychic "seventh sense" that enabled her to subconsciously anticipate an opponent's moves. While Rogue possessed Ms. Marvel's psyche, her "double" consciousness made her resistant to probes from even the most powerful telepaths.

After absorbing the powers of an alien Skrull, Rogue began to spontaneously reactivate previously imprinted abilities. Rogue could also tap into the residual psychic energy of those she had imprinted to determine their status and to relive past events from their perspective.

SPECIAL LIMITATIONS: Rogue previously could not come into skin-to-skin contact with another being without imprinting them. Remnants of the personalities of those who Rogue imprinted remained in her subconscious indefinitely. Certain powerful beings were able to supplant Rogue's personality, while others proved resistant to her power.

SPECIAL SKILLS: Rogue could formerly draw upon the combat and espionage training of Carol Danvers by granting control of her body to her alternate personality, a duplicate of Danvers'. Rogue can also speak fluent French.

POWER GRID

	1	2	3	4	5	6	7
INTELLIGENCE							
STRENGTH							
SPEED							
DURABILITY							
ENERGY PROJECTION							
FIGHTING SKILLS							

STORM

REAL NAME: Ororo Munroe
KNOWN ALIASES: "Beautiful Windrider", Mutate #20, White King
IDENTITY: Secret
OCCUPATION: Adventurer, former gladiator, thief, tribal patron
CITIZENSHIP: United States of America with no criminal record
PLACE OF BIRTH: New York City, New York
MARITAL STATUS: Single
KNOWN RELATIVES: Ashake (ancestor, deceased), David Munroe (father, deceased), N'dare Munroe (mother, deceased)
GROUP AFFILIATION: X-Men, formerly X-Treme Sanctions Executive, X-Treme X-Men, Tokyo Arena, Twelve, Morlocks (leader)
EDUCATION: College-level courses at Xavier's School

HISTORY: Ororo Munroe is a descendant of an ancient line of African priestesses, all of whom have white hair, blue eyes, and the potential to wield magic. She was born in Manhattan to her African princess mother, N'dare, and her American photojournalist father, David. Ororo was six months old when her family moved to Cairo, Egypt; five years later, tragedy struck during the Arab-Israeli conflict. A plane crashed into Ororo's home, killing her parents. Ororo survived, buried under rubble near her mother's body, and the resultant trauma left her with severe claustrophobia.

Ororo managed to escape with nothing but the tattered clothes on her back and her mother's ancestral ruby. Homeless and orphaned, Ororo was found by a gang of street urchins who took her to their master, Achmed el-Gibar. Ororo was trained in the arts of thievery, excelling in picking both pockets and locks. Soon after, Ororo picked the pocket of American tourist Charles Xavier, a powerful mutant telepath who used his abilities to stop the theft. At that moment, Xavier was psionically attacked by another mutant and Ororo used the opportunity to escape.

Years later, feeling a strong urge to wander south, Ororo left Cairo. During her travels, Ororo naïvely accepted a ride from a complete stranger who tried to hurt her. Forced to defend herself, Ororo killed the man; from that moment on, she swore never to take another human life.

Ororo wandered for thousands of miles, almost dying during her trek across the Sahara Desert. Her mutant ability to psionically control the weather emerged soon after, and she was able to use it to rescue T'Challa, a prince of the African nation of Wakanda, from would-be kidnappers. The pair spent much time together, however T'Challa's duties as a prince prevented them from further exploring their mutual attraction.

Finally, Ororo reached her ancestors' homeland on the Serengeti Plain in Kenya. She soon came to be the object of worship of the local tribes who believed her to be a goddess due to her gift. Years later, Ororo was forced to battle the threat of a fellow mutant weather manipulator known as Deluge, who sought revenge against humanity for persecuting him. With the help of several members of the team of mutant heroes known as the X-Men, Deluge was seemingly destroyed and Ororo returned to her life amongst the tribal people. The X-Men subsequently told their founder, Xavier, but he declined to contact Ororo at the time, not wanting to shock the young woman with the true nature of her powers.

Months later, however, Xavier was left with no choice but to recruit Storm and other mutants from around the world in order to rescue his original students from the sentient island-being Krakoa. Xavier explained to Ororo that she was not a "goddess", but a mutant, and as such she had a responsibility to use her abilities to help the world just as she had helped the local tribes. Curious, Ororo accepted Xavier's offer, and was given the codename "Storm".

After serving with the team for many years, Ororo was appointed leader of the team following the departure of former leader Cyclops. She was initially unsure about her new role, but with the support of her teammates Ororo soon became a capable leader. When Cyclops eventually returned to the team, Ororo once again doubted her leadership abilities after a mission she led went wrong. However, she soon asserted her position, reminding Cyclops that she was team leader.

Later, when the X-Men were captured and taken into space by the insectoid alien Brood race, Ororo fought back but her powers flared out of control. She discovered that she had been implanted with a Brood egg that would hatch and transform her into one of the aliens. Now wanting to unleash such an evil into the universe, Ororo attempted suicide by channelling all of the surrounding stellar energy into her own body, destroying the Brood embryo but leaving her drifting unprotected in space. She would have died if not for a member of the Acanti, a race of giant space-faring aliens that had been enslaved by the Brood. The Acanti that saved Ororo was the caretaker of his race's soul who had lost his mother and needed guidance. Ororo agreed to let her consciousness guide the young Acanti whilst it healed her damaged body, and, after the Brood were defeated, a restored Ororo returned home with the X-Men.

Soon after, the X-Men encountered the underground community of mutants known as the Morlocks who had kidnapped one of their former members, Angel. To save her friends, Ororo challenged the Morlock leader Callisto to a duel and bested her in hand-to-hand combat. As a result, Ororo became leader of the Morlocks and she ordered them to cease their hostilities against the surface-dwelling humans.

When the X-Men later travelled to Japan to attend the wedding of their team member Wolverine, Ororo first met the ninja named Yukio. A friend of Wolverine's, Yukio was the most care free spirit that Ororo had ever met and the two became fast friends. Yukio influenced a major rebellious change in Ororo's attitude towards life, and she took to wearing leather and shaved her hair into a Mohawk.

Ororo later had her powers accidentally neutralized by a gun invented by the mutant machinesmith named Forge, who took it upon himself to nurse Ororo back to health. During her convalescence, Ororo and Forge fell in love but their relationship was cut short after Ororo learned Forge had created the device that stripped her of her powers.

Ororo subsequently quit the X-Men and returned to Africa where she finally came to terms with losing her mutant ability. Returning to Cairo, Ororo joined Xavier's newest team of young mutants, the New Mutants, in an adventure into the past during which Ororo met one of her ancestors who helped the heroes return to their own time. Ororo and the New Mutants were subsequently captured by the Asgardian trickster god Loki, who sought to use her in one of his schemes to discredit his half-brother, the thunder god Thor, by restoring her abilities and brainwashing her into believing she was a goddess. With the aid of the X-Men, Ororo was able to reject Loki's gifts, thus thwarting his plan.

Ororo returned to the X-Men to find herself being challenged to a duel for leadership of the team by Cyclops. Despite her still being powerless, she won and Cyclops quit the team. Soon after, the X-Men and the Hellfire Club formed an alliance to combat the growing threats against mutants that saw Ororo share the position of White King with a reformed Magneto. The alliance was to be short-lived, however, after Ororo decided that in order to safeguard their friends and families from their many enemies, the X-Men must fake their deaths and become an underground proactive strike force. Soon Ororo realized that she needed her powers restored and so she sought out Forge for his help. She found Forge's old mentor Nazé instead, who informed her that Forge had been corrupted by his nemesis, the Adversary, and was seeking to destroy the world. Unbeknownst to Ororo, the Adversary had actually corrupted Nazé.

When Ororo finally located Forge, she found him atop a mountain seemingly opening a dimensional portal filled with demons. Ororo struck Forge down, and only then realized he had been attempting to close the portal, not open it. The Adversary then trapped Ororo and Forge in the other dimension and seized control of Dallas, warping time and space in order to foment chaos on Earth.

Ororo and Forge spent a year on an alternate Earth, during which time they made peace and admitted their love for one another. Forge used components from his cybernetic leg to fashion a new device that restored Ororo's powers, which she then used to energize a portal back to their own world. They rejoined the X-Men in time to defeat the Adversary, imprisoning him at the cost of their own lives. However, the Omniversal Guardian named Roma restored the X-Men to life, freeing the Adversary under the notion that there could be no order without chaos.

Soon after, Ororo was captured by the crazed scientist known as Nanny who sought to use Ororo's abilities in her quest to liberate the world's super-powered children by making orphans of them. Nanny used her technology to de-age Ororo to her pre-teens and strip her memories so as to better sway the mutant to her cause. However, Ororo fought back and overloaded Nanny's device. Once more a child with no memories of her life as an X-Man, the young-again Ororo returned to her life as a thief. On one caper, she found herself the target of the psychic being known as the Shadow King but was saved by a fellow mutant and thief named Gambit. The pair formed a partnership and, after Ororo regained her memories, she took Gambit to meet the X-Men.

Ororo was eventually restored to adulthood after agents of the island nation of Genosha captured the X-Men. Ororo underwent the Genoshan mutate transformation process, however the Genoshan Genegineer and Chief Magistrate were members of a rebel faction. They restored Ororo's body and mind, and the X-Men were able to defeat their aggressors.

Soon after, the X-Men were reformed into two separate strike teams, with Cyclops and Ororo as co-leaders. Forge aided both teams as their resident technician, however this left little time for them to rekindle their relationship. Forge still asked Ororo to marry him, but she hesitated on giving a reply. Forge was left thinking she did not truly love him and he left before she could respond with a "yes".

Months later, the eternal mutant Apocalypse made a bid for power by gathering together the Twelve, a group of mutants prophesied to usher in a golden age for their kind that counted Ororo amongst their number. Apocalypse was defeated, but not before the ultimate extent of Ororo's mutant power was revealed in an alternate future wherein she had evolved into a wholly elemental being.

Not long after, Ororo and five of her team mates formed a splinter group of X-Men, cutting all ties with the rest of the team to search for the diaries of the blind mutant seer Destiny that mapped the future of mutantkind. During a mission in Australia, Ororo was reunited with Gambit who sought to obtain her mother's ruby. It was revealed that the ruby was part of a set that, when empowered, could open a portal between dimensions. Several of the gems had already gone missing, and Gambit wished to ensure that Ororo's ruby remained safe. At that moment, the other-dimensional warrior named Shaitan attacked, capturing Gambit and stealing the ruby. Shaitan used the gems and Gambit's mutant ability to empower them, thus opening a portal allowing the armies of his master, Khan, to pass through and invade Earth.

Ororo's X-Men opposed the invaders, but she was seriously injured by Madripoor's ruling crimelord Viper and was subsequently taken prisoner by Khan himself. The warlord intended for Ororo to be his queen, and commanded his physicians to heal her. Ororo attempted to seduce Khan into calling off his invasion whilst her teammates fought to close the portal. Khan's other concubines grew jealous of Ororo's advances toward Khan and attempted to kill her. Despite her injuries, Ororo prevailed and escaped, rejoining her teammates as they destroyed the portal.

During her subsequent recuperation, which required her to undertake physical therapy to heal her back and legs, Ororo and

her team were asked back to the mansion to rejoin the core X-Men team. Ororo declined, however, believing that there was still work for her team to do. During a world summit to address the increasing hostilities between humans and mutants, Ororo offered her X-Men team's services to the United Nations as a global mutant police force, the X-Treme Sanctions Executive.

Ororo's first mission was a solo one as she was charged with infiltrating and exposing an underground slave trading network in Japan that forced mutants to fight in gladiator-style arenas. Soon after, Ororo and her team returned to Westchester to help rebuild the mansion following an attack by Magneto. Ororo and her teammates then rejoined the core X-Men team and continue to function as representatives of the U.N.

PHYSICAL DESCRIPTION:

HEIGHT: 5'11"
WEIGHT: 127 lbs
EYES: Blue
HAIR: White

DISTINGUISHING FEATURES: None

POWERS & ABILITIES:

STRENGTH LEVEL: Storm possesses the normal human strength of a woman of her age, height, and build who engages in intensive regular exercise.

SUPERHUMAN POWERS: Storm is a mutant who possesses the psionic ability to manipulate weather patterns over limited areas. She can stimulate the creation of any form of precipitation, such as rain or fog; generate winds in varying degrees of intensity up to and including hurricane force; raise or lower the humidity and temperature in her immediate vicinity; induce lightning and other electrical atmospheric phenomena; and disperse natural storms so as to create clear change. Storm can direct the path of certain atmospheric effects, such as bolts of lightning, with her hands.

Storm's control over the atmosphere is such that she can create certain effects over a specific area while shielding smaller areas within that region. For example, she can create a rainstorm around herself but prevent the raindrops from touching her. Storm can also create atmospheric phenomena over very small areas, such as a rainstorm small enough to water a single potted plant.

Storm can only manipulate weather patterns as they exist naturally. For example, she can end a drought in one area by creating torrential rains there, but that would necessitate robbing all available moisture from the surrounding areas. Storm is not able to create atmospheric conditions that do not exist naturally on the planet she is on. For example, Storm is unable to lower temperatures as far as absolute zero or raise them to solar intensities while on Earth.

The limit to the size of the area over which Storm can manipulate the weather is not yet known. However, she once diverted the jet stream so as to create storms over the entire East Coast of the United States. She can create weather effects within indoor areas or within artificially maintained environments. Storm is limited by the force of her will and the

strength of her body. It once took her several hours to stop a savage blizzard sweeping over much of Canada, and she nearly died from exhaustion in the process.

Storm is able to fly by creating winds strong enough to support her weight and to propel her forward through the air. Storm can thus travel as fast as any wind can, and has reached speeds up to 300 miles per hour. She can also summon winds strong enough to propel others aloft. Storm's powers over the atmosphere enable her to breathe at any speed, protect her from air friction, and grant her limited immunity to extreme heat and cold.

Storm is also able to alter her visual perception so as to perceive electrical energy patterns as well as those factors responsible for existing meteorological phenomena in her surrounding environment.

SPECIAL LIMITATIONS: Storm's ability to manipulate the weather in her immediate vicinity is affected by her emotions; hence, if she does not maintain control, a fit of rage might induce a destructive storm. Storm also suffers from severe claustrophobia.

SPECIAL SKILLS: Storm is extraordinarily skilled at picking both locks and pockets. Storm is also a gifted hand-to-hand combatant, having been trained extensively by her fellow X-Man Wolverine, and is also an excellent marksman.

PARAPHERNALIA:

OTHER ACCESSORIES: Storm often carries a set of lockpicks on her person.

POWER GRID	1	2	3	4	5	6	7
INTELLIGENCE							
STRENGTH							
SPEED							
DURABILITY							
ENERGY PROJECTION							
FIGHTING SKILLS							

PURPOSE: Experimentation on superhumans to create super-soldiers; ultimate elimination of all mutants except those deemed useable

KNOWN LEADERS: John Sublime, Professor Thorton, Director Colcord, Director Jackson

KNOWN SCIENTIFIC STAFF: Doctor Cornelius, Carol Hines, Doctor Killebrew, Doctor Horatio Huxley, Doctor Charles Windsor, Doctor Duncan, Doctor Zira, Doctor Vapor

KNOWN AGENTS: Wolverine, Sabretooth, Maverick/Agent Zero, Mastodon, Wraith, Silver Fox, Vole, Wildcat, Psi-Borg, Ajax, Kane, Sluggo, Slayback, Deadpool, Copycat, Mesmero, Sauron, Wild Child, Aurora, Washout, Jack in the Box, Madison Jeffries, Marrow, Wildside, Reaper, Chamber

MAJOR ENEMIES: Wolverine, Cable, Maverick/Agent Zero, X-Men

KNOWN BASES OF OPERATIONS: Weapon X Facility, Alberta, Canada; Neverland

KNOWN EXTENT OF OPERATIONS: Worldwide

FIRST APPEARANCE: Marvel Comics Presents #72 (1991)

HISTORY: The origins of the clandestine Weapon X Program date back to 1945 when a civilian advisor to the American military named Thorton investigated a liberated concentration camp and discovered the hidden laboratory of the enigmatic geneticist Mister Sinister. Using Sinister's research as the basis for his own work, Thorton, also known simply as the Professor, formed the Weapon Plus Program at the behest of the U.S. government. Absorbing the resources of earlier projects such as Operation: Rebirth, which was retroactively designated Weapon I, Weapon Plus was dedicated to creating super-soldiers. Over the next decade and a half, the Program went through various stages of development. The Weapon II and III Programs used animals as test subjects, while Weapons IV, V, and VI experimented upon various ethnic minorities. Beginning with Weapon VII, superhuman mutants became the preferred test subjects, a trend which continued from Weapon VIII through Weapon IX. The Professor remained active as a scientist throughout these incarnations of Weapon Plus, only to be repeatedly passed up for promotion.

By the 1960s, the Program had advanced to Weapon X and operated under the auspices of the Central Intelligence Agency. Several mutant operatives were organized as the covert operations unit Team X, including Wolverine, Sabretooth, Maverick, Wraith, Mastodon, and Silver Fox. The members of Team X were implanted with false memories by Psi-Borg, a telepathic ally of the Program, with the ultimate intent of suppressing their true memories and awareness of their abilities to become sleeper agents. A separate branch of the program, the Shiva Scenario, was designed to dispatch heavily armored robots to kill any operatives that went rogue. Team X members also received age suppression and healing factor treatments based on Wolverine's own mutant nature. By the early 1970s, Team X had been disbanded, with only Wraith and Maverick remaining in government service. The Weapon X Program continued operations under the cover of a division of the U.S. Department of Agriculture.

Over a decade later, the U.S. and Canadian governments were jointly administrating the Weapon X Program, with its Canadian branch in turn jointly operated by Canada's Department K and Department H. In this incarnation, Weapon X oversaw the enhancement of various Canadian government operatives, both human and mutant. One such operative was Wade Wilson, who received an artificial healing factor based on the one possessed by Wolverine. The Program was less than successful as most of the participants suffered from various physical or mental breakdowns and were sent to a special Hospice, where, unknown to the Canadian government, scientist Doctor Killebrew conducted inhumane experiments in his Workshop with his assistant, the Attending. Killebrew's activities were disrupted when Wilson, calling himself Deadpool, led a massive breakout; Canada eventually shut down its Weapon X branch.

the Professor, assisted by Doctor Cornelius, Carol Hines, and the manipulative John Sublime. Guided by an unidentified backer, the Professor chose Wolverine as his first test subject. Logan was kidnapped and taken to a Canadian facility where he was subjected to a brutal process in which the near-indestructible metal Adamantium was bonded to his skeleton, including his mutant claws. The Professor was surprised at the full extent of Logan's mutant nature, which enabled him to recover from the process far more rapidly than anticipated. Reduced to a quasi-mindless state, Wolverine was sent to slaughter the inhabitants of the small town of Roanoke as a test of his abilities. He ultimately broke free of the Professor's conditioning and ran amok in the Weapon X facility. In the course of his escape, he slew most of the facility's personnel and savagely butchered a guard named Malcolm Colcord. Miraculously, Colcord survived, but kept his scarred face as a visual reminder of his hatred for Wolverine.

Logan was subsequently found by Department H's director James Hudson and his wife Heather, who nursed him back to health; he soon joined the Department as both an espionage agent and, later, a costumed operative. His memories of Weapon X clouded by memory implants and his own horrendous experience, he apparently did not recognize the significance of the term when, either by accident or design, it was used as his codename.

Despite the fiasco of Wolverine's escape, Weapon X continued under the Professor's guidance, while his associate Sublime moved on to later incarnations of the Weapon Plus Program. Eventually threatened with a shutdown, the Professor had Weapon X break all ties with Weapon Plus.

Art by Barry Windsor-Smith

In recent years, Wolverine's memory of his manipulation at the hands of the Weapon X Program began to return, resulting in his being targeted by a Shiva unit. After fighting his way past the robot, he sought the Professor, only to find that he had been slain by Silver Fox, now a high-ranking operative of the terrorist organization Hydra. With his death, Weapon X was apparently abandoned, as Weapon Plus had long since superceded it. The Professor's associates, Cornelius and Hines, died shortly afterward at the hands of Maverick and Psi-Borg, respectively. Sometime later, Doctor Horatio Huxley attempted to revive Canada's Weapon X branch with a new test subject whom he exposed to deadly bacteria in hope of controlling the world, but after battling Canada's super-team Alpha Flight, the new Weapon X sacrificed his life to prevent the bacteria from spreading.

Meanwhile, Sublime, now the head of the Weapon Plus Program, contacted Colcord and encouraged him to lobby for the reopening of the U.S. Weapon X Program. Colcord was successful, and became the Program's new Director with renegade S.H.I.E.L.D. agent Brent Jackson as his second-in-command. Colcord's plan was to openly recruit mutants, particularly those with disfigurements or poorly controlled powers, with the promise of treating them in return for their service in various field assignments.

Investigating the resources of the Program's earlier incarnation, Colcord discovered the means by which Wolverine had previously been mentally controlled, and directed his nemesis in stalking former operatives, who were either recruited or slain by Colcord's forces. Among the first to rejoin was Wolverine's nemesis, the feral mutant Sabretooth. Wolverine ultimately broke free of Colcord's control but was captured and held in a Program facility. He was freed by the mysterious mercenary the Shiver Man, and Colcord, unwilling to risk a further encounter, teleported himself and his staff away.

Colcord subsequently recruited several other operatives for Weapon X, all of whom he equipped with implants preventing them from turning upon him or other high-ranking personnel. Colcord then opened the Neverland concentration camp, designed by the brainwashed mutant metalsmith Madison Jeffries, where mutants who were deemed useful were utilized as support staff and those who were not were executed.

Weapon X's activities came to the attention of the mutant time-traveler Cable, who organized an underground movement to oppose them. However, Jackson, betraying Colcord, manipulated Cable's resistance into storming the Weapon X facility, forcing Colcord to flee, only for Jackson to betray Cable's forces in return. Jackson was soon made the new Director, but he remained unaware that one of the scientists stationed at Neverland, Doctor Charles Windsor, was in fact a disguised Mister Sinister, ironically using this outgrowth of his past work to further his experiments.

Subsequently, Wolverine's current team, the mutant adventurers the X-Men, arranged for one of their members, Chamber, to infiltrate Weapon X. Accepted as a field agent, Chamber was assigned by Jackson to kill Sublime. Meanwhile, operative Agent Zero, the former Team X alumnus Maverick, turned renegade and began single-handedly targeting former operative Marrow's new, more violent version of Cable's underground. At the same time, Colcord, driven to madness by his situation, plotted an assault upon mutantkind with an army of Jeffries-built Sentinel robots.

After Chamber went missing while seeking to discover the nature of Neverland's activities, Wolverine set out to find him but instead found the camp abandoned. Zero found the Weapon X facility similarly vacant, and both men joined forces with Fantomex, formerly Weapon XIII of the Weapon Plus Program, in search of answers. However, they found only Sublime, who had survived Chamber's attack, and the three barely escaped an attack by Sublime's mutated U-Men soldiers. Wolverine and Zero later defeated Fantomex after he was found to still be under Weapon Plus control.

Wolverine then found himself in conflict with an offshoot of Weapon X in pursuit of another former Weapon X experimentee, the female feral mutant called the Native. Aided by Sabretooth, who sought revenge on this group's leaders for their betrayal of him, Wolverine was able to rescue the Native. Escaping into the nearby woods, the Native was subsequently hunted down and slain by Sabretooth.

SUBLIME
(John Sublime)
Weapon Plus overseer
FIRST APPEARANCE: New X-Men 2001 Annual (2001)

PROFESSOR
(Thorton, first name unrevealed)
Former Weapon X director
FIRST APPEARANCE: Marvel Comics Presents #72 (1991)
FIRST ACTIVE: Marvel Comics Presents #72 (1991)
LAST APPEARANCE: Wolverine Vol. 2 #50 (1992)

DOCTOR CORNELIUS
(first name unrevealed)
Former head scientist
FIRST APPEARANCE: Marvel Comics Presents #73 (1991)
FIRST ACTIVE: Marvel Comics Presents #73 (1991)
LAST APPEARANCE: X-Men Vol. 2 #7 (1992)

CAROL HINES
Former laboratory assistant
FIRST APPEARANCE: Marvel Comics Presents #73 (1991)
FIRST ACTIVE: Marvel Comics Presents #73 (1991)
LAST APPEARANCE: Wolverine Vol. 2 #63 (1992)

WOLVERINE
(James Howlett/Logan)
Former field agent
FIRST APPEARANCE: Incredible Hulk Vol. 2 #180 (1974)
FIRST ACTIVE: Marvel Comics Presents #72 (1991)

SABRETOOTH
(Victor Creed)
Former field agent
FIRST APPEARANCE: Iron Fist Vol. 1 #14 (1977)
FIRST ACTIVE: Wolverine Vol. 2 #48 (1991)

MAVERICK/AGENT ZERO
(Christoph Nord)
Former field agent
FIRST APPEARANCE: (as Maverick) X-Men Vol. 2 #5 (1992), (as Agent Zero) Weapon X: The Draft - Agent Zero #1 (2002)
FIRST ACTIVE: (as Maverick) X-Men Vol. 2 #5 (1992), (as Agent Zero) Weapon X: The Draft - Agent Zero #1 (2002)

MASTODON
Former field agent
FIRST APPEARANCE: Wolverine Vol. 2 #48 (1991)
LAST APPEARANCE: Wolverine Vol. 2 #61 (1992)

WRAITH
(John Carlisle)
Former field agent
FIRST APPEARANCE: Wolverine Vol. 2 #60 (1992)
FIRST ACTIVE: Wolverine Vol. 2 #60 (1992)
LAST APPEARANCE: Wolverine Vol. 2 #166 (2001)

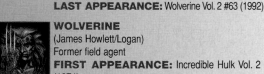

SILVER FOX
Former field agent
FIRST APPEARANCE: Wolverine Vol. 2 #10 (1989)
FIRST ACTIVE: Wolverine Vol. 2 #48 (1991)
LAST APPEARANCE: Wolverine Vol. 2 #64 (1992)

PSI-BORG
(Aldo Ferro)
Former debriefing specialist
FIRST APPEARANCE: Wolverine Vol. 2 #62 (1992)
FIRST ACTIVE: Wolverine Vol. 2 #62 (1992)
LAST APPEARANCE: Wolverine Vol. 2 #64 (1992)

DEADPOOL
(Jack/Wade Wilson)
Former field agent
FIRST APPEARANCE: New Mutants Vol. 1 #98 (1991)
FIRST ACTIVE: Marvel Comics 1998 Annual Starring Deadpool and Death (1998)

DOCTOR KILLEBREW
Former Workshop scientist
FIRST APPEARANCE: Deadpool Vol. 1 #1 (1994)
FIRST ACTIVE: Marvel Comics 1998 Annual Starring Deadpool and Death (1998)
LAST APPEARANCE: Deadpool Vol. 2 #19 (1998)

THE ATTENDING/AJAX
(Francis, full name unrevealed)
Former Hospice enforcer
FIRST APPEARANCE: Deadpool Vol. 2 #14 (1998)
FIRST ACTIVE: Marvel Comics 1998 Annual Starring Deadpool and Death (1998)
LAST APPEARANCE: Deadpool Vol. 2 #19 (1998)

DIRECTOR
(Malcolm Colcord
Former Weapon X leader
FIRST APPEARANCE: (in shadow) Wolverine Vol. 2 #160 (2001), (fully) Wolverine Vol. 2 #166 (2001)
FIRST ACTIVE: Wolverine Vol. 2 #160 (2001)

JACKSON, BRENT
Current Weapon X leader
FIRST APPEARANCE: Wolverine Vol. 2 #163 (2001)
FIRST ACTIVE: Wolverine Vol. 2 #166 (2001)

**MISTER SINISTER/
DOCTOR CHARLES WINDSOR**
(Nathaniel Essex)
Former head scientist
FIRST APPEARANCE: (as Mister Sinister) Uncanny X-Men #213 (1987), (as Windsor) Wolverine Vol. 2 #173 (2002)
FIRST ACTIVE: Wolverine Vol. 2 #173 (2002)

AURORA
(Jeanne-Marie Beaubier)
Former field agent
FIRST APPEARANCE: X-Men Vol. 1 #120 (1979)
FIRST ACTIVE: Weapon X: The Draft - Wild Child #1 (2002)

KANE
(Garrison Kane)
Former field agent
FIRST APPEARANCE: X-Force Vol. 1 #2 (1991)
FIRST ACTIVE: Deadpool Vol. 2 #57 (2001)
LAST APPEARANCE: Weapon X Vol. 2 #12 (2003)

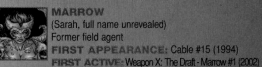

MARROW
(Sarah, full name unrevealed)
Former field agent
FIRST APPEARANCE: Cable #15 (1994)
FIRST ACTIVE: Weapon X: The Draft - Marrow #1 (2002)

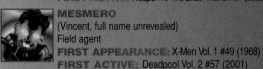

MESMERO
(Vincent, full name unrevealed)
Field agent
FIRST APPEARANCE: X-Men Vol. 1 #49 (1968)
FIRST ACTIVE: Deadpool Vol. 2 #57 (2001)

SAURON
(Karl Lykos)
Field agent
FIRST APPEARANCE: X-Men Vol. 1 #59 (1963)
FIRST ACTIVE: Deadpool Vol. 2 #57 (2001)

WILD CHILD
(Kyle Gibney)
Field agent
FIRST APPEARANCE: Alpha Flight Vol. 1 #1 (1983)
FIRST ACTIVE: Deadpool Vol. 2 #57 (2001)

WASHOUT
(John Lopez)
Former field agent
FIRST APPEARANCE: X-Force Vol. 1 #129 (2002)
FIRST ACTIVE: Weapon X Vol. 2 #1/2 (2002)
LAST APPEARANCE: Weapon X Vol. 2 #11 (2003)

JACK IN THE BOX
(Jack, full name unrevealed)
Former Neverland staff
FIRST APPEARANCE: Weapon X: The Draft - Sauron #1 (2002)
FIRST ACTIVE: Weapon X: The Draft - Sauron #1 (2002)

JEFFRIES, MADISON
Former technical support
FIRST APPEARANCE: Alpha Flight Vol. 1 #1 (1983)
FIRST ACTIVE: Weapon X Vol. 2 #1 (2002)

WILDSIDE
(Richard Gill)
Former field agent
FIRST APPEARANCE: New Mutants Vol. 1 #87 (1990)
FIRST ACTIVE: Weapon X Vol. 2 #5 (2003)

REAPER
(Pantu Hurageb)
Former field agent
FIRST APPEARANCE: New Mutants Vol. 1 #87 (1990)
FIRST ACTIVE: Weapon X Vol. 2 #5 (2003)

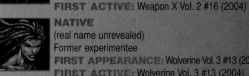

CHAMBER
(Jonothon Starsmore)
Former field agent
FIRST APPEARANCE: Generation X #1 (1994)
FIRST ACTIVE: Weapon X Vol. 2 #16 (2004)

NATIVE
(real name unrevealed)
Former experimentee
FIRST APPEARANCE: Wolverine Vol. 3 #13 (2004)
FIRST ACTIVE: Wolverine Vol. 3 #13 (2004)
LAST APPEARANCE: Wolverine Vol. 3 #19 (2004)

DOCTOR VAPOR
Former scientist
FIRST APPEARANCE: Wolverine Vol. 3 #17 (2004)
FIRST ACTIVE: Wolverine Vol. 3 #17 (2004)
LAST APPEARANCE: Wolverine Vol. 3 #18 (2004)

REAL NAME: James Howlett
KNOWN ALIASES: Logan, formerly Weapon Ten, Mai'keth, Death, Mutate #9601, Jim Logan, Patch, Canucklehead, Emilio Garra, Weapon Chi, Weapon X, Experiment X, Agent Ten, Canada, Wildboy, Peter Richards, others
IDENTITY: Secret
OCCUPATION: Adventurer, former bartender, bouncer, spy, government operative, mercenary, soldier, sailor, miner, various others
CITIZENSHIP: Canada with no known criminal record
PLACE OF BIRTH: Alberta, Canada
MARITAL STATUS: Divorced (Viper)

KNOWN RELATIVES: Unnamed grandfather (deceased), John Howlett Sr. (father, deceased), Elizabeth Howlett (mother, deceased), Daniel Howlett (brother, deceased), Viper (ex-wife), Amiko (foster daughter), Erista (son), X-23 (clone)
GROUP AFFILIATION: X-Men, formerly Horsemen of Apocalypse, Fantastic Four, Secret Defenders, Clan Yashida, Department H, First Flight, Department K, Weapon X, Canadian Army
EDUCATION: Unrevealed

HISTORY: Born into privilege in Alberta, Canada during the late 19th Century, James Howlett was the second son of wealthy landowner John Howlett and his wife, Elizabeth. After the untimely death of his elder brother, Daniel, the sickly James became close friends with Rose, a governess living at the Howlett estate, and the young boy known only as "Dog", the son of the Howletts' cruel groundskeeper, Thomas Logan.

Dog's growing obsession with Rose prompted him to attack her one day, forcing James' father to fire Thomas and evict him and Dog from their home on the estate. Unbeknownst to John, Thomas was having an affair with Elizabeth, and he sought to convince her to leave with them. When John interrupted their discussion, Thomas shot and killed him. The shock of seeing his father murdered, caused James to manifest his latent mutant abilities when bone claws jutted from the back of each of his hands. He attacked and killed Thomas, and slashed Dog's face. Completely unhinged by the violence, Elizabeth took her own life.

James suffered a severe breakdown, but his mutant healing factor "repaired" his mind, blocking all memories of the traumatic events at the estate. With James now wanted for murder, Rose spirited him away to a mining colony in British Columbia and gave him the name "Logan" to protect his true identity. The frail "Logan" grew into a strapping young man at the mine, and acquired the nickname "Wolverine" thanks to his tenacity and refusal to back down from a challenge. Logan's happiness at the camp came to an end when Dog tracked him down. Remembering the night of his father's death, Logan fought Dog savagely. During the struggle, Logan accidentally impaled Rose on his claws. Wracked by grief over the death of his first true love, Logan fled into the woods and was not seen again for some time.

Eventually, Logan came to reside in a frontier community nestled in the Canadian Rockies. Among the community's residents was a man who would become his greatest foe – Victor Creed, better known as Sabretooth. Logan had fallen in love with a young Native American girl named Silver Fox, but their happiness was short-lived after she was brutally attacked by Sabretooth on Logan's birthday. Logan sought to avenge his lover's apparent death, but was easily defeated by the older and more experienced mutant. Unable to bear the pain of both his loss and his defeat, Logan left the community.

Some time later, Logan joined the Canadian Army and fought in World War I as a member of the Devil's Brigade. He eventually left the military and travelled to China where he first met Ogun, a Japanese samurai and sorcerer who began instructing the young mutant in the martial arts. Logan remained under Ogun's tutelage for many years, eventually leaving to adventure on the island nation of Madripoor. At the advent of World War II, Logan worked with the American super-soldier Captain America in opposing the Nazi agent Baron Strucker and The Hand ninja clan. Soon after, Logan returned to Canada and once again joined the Army. Attaining the rank of Corporal, he was assigned to the First Canadian Parachute Battalion and fought at the Battle of Normandy.

After the war, Logan was recruited into Weapon X, a multinational intelligence operation overseen by the American Central Intelligence

Art by Sean Chen

Agency. Amongst his teammates, Logan was surprised to encounter both his nemesis Sabretooth and his former lover Silver Fox. The program used various methods, including false memory implants, to ensure the loyalty of its members despite their past affiliations. As a result, Logan was paired with Sabretooth on numerous missions.

Logan eventually quit Team X and worked for a time as a spy for the secret branch of the Canadian government known as Department K. Some time later, Logan was captured and taken back to Weapon X with the intent of using him in an experiment that would bond the nigh-indestructible metal Adamantium to his skeleton. Forced to undergo the procedure, Logan was subsequently brainwashed in an attempt to create the perfect assassin. However, Logan rebelled against Weapon X's programming and slipped into a berzerk fury, killing almost everyone in the complex before fleeing into the nearby woods. James Hudson and his wife Heather eventually discovered Logan in a feral state and brought him back to humanity. He then helped James form The Flight, the first team of super-powered adventurers that operated under the auspices of the Canadian government's Department H.

On his first public mission for the Department, Logan was sent to capture the gamma-spawned creature known as the Hulk, and clashed with both the jade giant and the mythical beast known as the Wendigo. Logan was subsequently approached by the telepathic mutant Professor Charles Xavier, founder of the team of mutant heroes known as the X-Men. Xavier was recruiting mutants to help rescue from the sentient island-being Krakoa. Logan resigned his commission with Department H and accompanied Xavier to rescue the X-Men. Afterwards, he joined the team if only for his attraction to one of its members, Jean Grey.

During one mission with the X-Men to Japan, Logan met the Lady Mariko Yashida, cousin of the former X-Man Sunfire. At first frightened of him, Logan was soon able to put Mariko at ease, and he found himself strongly attracted to her gentle, refined manner. They spent much time together during the X-Men's stay in Japan, and later, when she visited New York, they continued their relationship.

On a return visit to Japan, Logan discovered that Mariko's father, the crimelord Shingen Harada, had forced her to marry one of his criminal associates who proved to be an abusive husband. Logan sought to convince Mariko to leave with him, but she was bound by her duty to her father to remain. Shingen sought to eliminate Logan, and employed the ninja named Yukio to capture him. Drugged with nerve poison, Logan was brought before Shingen who challenged him to a duel while Mariko watched. Unaware that her father, by striking at Logan's sensitive pressure points, was actually trying to kill him, Mariko was shocked when Logan retaliated by lashing out at Shingen with his claws. Noticing Mariko's dismay, Logan lost the will to battle and was soundly defeated. Disillusioned, Mariko agreed with her father that Logan was unworthy of her love.

Logan later returned for Mariko, and slew Shingen after his dishonorable actions were revealed. As the new head of Clan Yashida, Mariko named Logan as her champion and presented him with the Clan's honor sword. They then announced their engagement, however Mariko called the wedding off whilst under the influence of the psychic mutant Mastermind. He also forced Mariko to establish ties between her Clan and the Japanese underworld. After Mastermind was defeated, Mariko was deeply

ashamed by what she had done while under his control and vowed that she could not marry Logan until she had proven herself worthy to him.

During the X-Men's next mission in Japan, Logan encountered a dying woman who made him promise to care for her daughter, Amiko. Logan agreed; realizing his life was not one to share with a young girl, he left Amiko in Mariko's care. Furthermore, in exchange for the honor sword of the Clan Yashida, Mariko's half-brother – Keniuchio Harada, the Silver Samurai – became honor-bound to ensure Amiko's welfare.

Later, after a battle with the X-Men's nemesis Magneto, the mutant master of magnetism, Logan and his teammates found themselves in the hidden Antarctic jungle known as the Savage Land. Finding himself at home in the prehistoric surroundings, Logan would come to be a regular visitor over the ensuing years. He even fathered a son with a Savage Land native named Gahck.

Logan began regularly visiting Madripoor once more, buying in to one of the local establishments, the Princess Bar. He continued to adventure with the X-Men until an encounter in Australia with the band of cybernetic assassins known as the Reavers. Captured and crucified, Logan was freed by the young mutant named Jubilee, who escaped with him to Madripoor. During his recovery, Logan came to regard Jubilee as something of a daughter and the unlikely duo shared several adventures before rejoining the X-Men.

Eventually locating the hidden facility of the Weapon X project, Logan learned of his false memory implants and, after the members of Team X were reluctantly reunited, they tracked down the man responsible and defeated him. Soon after, on another visit to Japan, Logan was present when a Hand assassin wounded Mariko with an incurable toxin. She begged him to end her pain, and seeing no other alternative he acceded to her request with his claws. To this day, Logan visits Mariko's grave on the anniversary of her death each year to pay his respects.

During another encounter with Magneto, Logan was critically injured when the Adamantium was forcibly removed from his body. His healing factor overloaded as it worked to repair the massive trauma, but Logan still prevailed. During his recuperation, Logan rediscovered the full extent of his mutant nature as he unsheathed claws of bone. He then left the X-Men for a time, briefly returning to watch the wedding of his former teammates Cyclops to Jean Grey from afar.

Logan was later kidnapped by Genesis, pretender to the legacy of the eternal mutant Apocalypse, who sought to make Logan one of his Horsemen by recreating the Adamantium bonding process. This time, however, Logan's body rejected the Adamantium, and he regressed once more into a feral state. With the help of the ninja named Elektra, Logan found his way back onto the path to humanity.

Logan was then forced to follow his code of giri, or "honorable debt," when he reluctantly agreed to marry the crimelord known as the Viper which allowed her to take control of Madripoor. Logan was later seemingly killed in battle against the newest Horseman of Apocalypse to bear the name Death, however it was revealed that a member of the shape-shifting alien Skrulls had impersonated him. Logan had actually been captured by Apocalypse and transformed into Death, complete with a new Adamantium skeleton. Logan eventually managed to break Apocalypse's programming and rejoined the X-Men once more.

Logan's past would come back to haunt him once more when the Weapon X program was reactivated and began recruiting many of its former agents, including Sabretooth. However, Sabretooth had his own agenda, and used the program's technology to strip Logan of his mutant powers. Sabretooth then recruited Logan's enemies to attack his closest friends. Although powerless, Logan confronted Sabretooth in the original Weapon X facility, but was no match for him and was left for dead.

However, Logan survived once more and soon after learned the truth behind the Weapon X program from the mercenary named Fantomex. Weapon X was but one of a series of experimental programs, collectively known as the Weapon Plus program, which began with the "creation" of America's original super-soldier, Captain America. The program sought to create an army of super-soldiers to protect mankind against the perceived threat posed by mutants. Logan was involved in the tenth attempt, while Fantomex was part of the thirteenth.

Whilst investigating the orbital Weapon Plus facility known as The World, Fantomex gave Logan access to a computer file that, at long last, revealed the mysteries of his past. Logan's discovery was interrupted by the arrival of the program's latest creation, Weapon XV. Logan managed to defeat the creature, but the battle damaged the base and he was left stranded in space. Sensing Logan was in danger, Jean Grey took a shuttle to return him to Earth but the pair were trapped on Avalon, Magneto's former space station, which the villain sent hurtling into the sun. Only Jean's transformation into the cosmic entity known as the Phoenix saved them, and they returned to Earth to rejoin the X-Men in opposing Magneto. In the ensuing battle, Magneto killed Jean with a lethal electromagnetic pulse. This act sent Logan into a berserk rage, and he decapitated Magneto. When Xavier announced his intent to return Magneto to his nation of Genosha for a proper burial, Logan followed. The two argued over their differing opinions of Magneto, resulting in Logan leaving on less than friendly terms.

PHYSICAL DESCRIPTION:

HEIGHT: 5'3"
WEIGHT: (w/o Adamantium) 195 lbs., (w/ Adamantium) 300 lbs.
EYES: Black
HAIR: Black

DISTINGUISHING FEATURES: Fang-like canine teeth, hirsute, unique hairstyle.

POWERS & ABILITIES:

STRENGTH LEVEL: Wolverine possesses the normal human strength of a man of his apparent age, height, and build who engages in intensive regular exercise.

SUPERHUMAN POWERS: Wolverine is a mutant with the ability to regenerate damaged or destroyed areas of his cellular structure at a rate far greater than an ordinary human. The speed at which this healing factor works varies in direct proportion to the severity of the damage suffered. For example, Wolverine can fully recover from a normal gunshot

wound in a non-vital area of his body within an hour. More serious injuries can take months to fully heal.

Wolverine's healing factor also affords him virtual immunity to poisons and most drugs, as well as an enhanced resistance to diseases. For example, it is nearly impossible for him to become intoxicated from drinking alcohol. He also has a limited immunity to the fatigue poisons generated by bodily activity, and hence he has greater endurance than an ordinary human. Also due to his healing factor, Wolverine has an extended life span.

Wolverine also has superhumanly acute senses, allowing him to see things at a distance greater than that of a normal human. His sense of smell is similarly enhanced, allowing him to recognize people and objects by scent, even if they are hidden from sight. Wolverine can use his enhanced senses to track any creature with an impressive degree of success.

Furthermore, Wolverine possesses six retractable one-foot-long bone claws, three in each arm, that are housed beneath the skin and muscle of his forearms. At will, Wolverine can release these slightly curved claws through his skin beneath the knuckles on each hand. The skin between the knuckles tears and bleeds, but is quickly repaired by his healing factor.

Wolverine can unsheathe any number of his claws at once; however he must keep his wrists straight at the moment his claws shoot from his forearms into his hands. When unsheathed, the claws reside in his hands and thus Wolverine can still bend his wrists. The claws are naturally sharp and tougher than that of normal human bone structure.

SPECIAL LIMITATIONS: Despite the extent of his healing factor, Wolverine is not immortal. If the injuries are extensive enough, especially if they result in the loss of vital organs, large amounts of blood, oxygen deprivation, and/or loss of physical form, Wolverine can die.

SPECIAL SKILLS: Due to his extensive training as a soldier, a C.I.A. operative, a Samurai, a member of the Weapon X program, and the X-Men, Wolverine is a master of multiple forms of martial arts, weapons, and vehicles. He is also a trained expert in explosives, espionage, and assassination. Wolverine is also fluent in many languages, including Japanese, Russian, Chinese, Cheyenne, Lakota, and Spanish. He also has some knowledge of French, Thai, and Vietnamese.

PARAPHERNALIA:

PERSONAL WEAPONRY: The nigh-indestructible metal Adamantium has been artificially bonded to Wolverine's entire skeleton. As a result, his bones are virtually unbreakable and his claws are capable of cutting through almost any substance, depending on its thickness and the amount of force he can exert. Due to his healing factor, the presence of Adamantium in his body does not interfere with his bones' normal function of generating blood corpuscles.

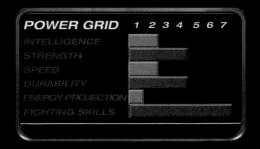

POWER GRID | 1 2 3 4 5 6 7
INTELLIGENCE
STRENGTH
SPEED
DURABILITY
ENERGY PROJECTION
FIGHTING SKILLS

HISTORY: Under a cloud of increasing anti-mutant sentiment, Professor Xavier created a safe haven at his Westchester mansion where he could train young mutants to use their powers for the betterment of mankind. Aided by F.B.I. agent Fred Duncan, Xavier spent months recruiting his early students (code-named Cyclops, Iceman, Angel, Beast and Marvel Girl), dubbing them "X-Men" because each possessed an "extra" ability normal humans lacked. The X-Men made their public debut by thwarting Magneto's seizure of the Cape Citadel missile base. The U.S. military was grateful, and the youngsters were initially regarded as heroes. Magneto would battle the X-Men repeatedly over the years, sometimes leading his Brotherhood of Evil Mutants. The X-Men also battled such threats as the immovable Blob, the untouchable Unus, the alien Lucifer, the savage Swamp Men, the enigmatic Stranger, the unstoppable Juggernaut, and the giant mutant-hunting Sentinel robots.

The arrogant mutated human Mimic briefly joined the team before Xavier secretly went into hiding. Requiring seclusion to prepare for a forthcoming invasion of Earth by the alien Z'nox, Xavier had the shape-shifting mutant Changeling impersonate him in order to supervise the X-Men in his absence; however, the Changeling "Xavier" died heroically in battle against the subterranean Grotesk. Of the X-Men, only Marvel Girl knew that Xavier was still alive, though she was sworn to secrecy. Duncan had the X-Men disband briefly, but the team had regrouped by the time Xavier finally came out of hiding, leading them in repelling the Z'nox with the aid of the Fantastic Four. Joined by Polaris and Havok, the heroes befriended Avia of the Savage Land's Nhu-Gari race, and fought the likes of African mutant Deluge (alongside young future member Storm), the

CURRENT MEMBERS: Beast (Henry McCoy), Bishop (Lucas Bishop), Colossus (Piotr Rasputin), Cyclops (Scott Summers), Gambit (Remy LeBeau), Havok (Alex Summers), Iceman (Robert Drake), Lockheed, Marvel Girl/Phoenix (Rachel Grey), Nightcrawler (Kurt Wagner), Polaris (Lorna Dane), Psylocke (Elisabeth Braddock), Shadowcat/Sprite/Ariel (Kitty Pryde), Rogue (Anna Marie), Storm (Ororo Munroe), White Queen (Emma Frost), Wolverine (James Howlett)

FORMER MEMBERS: Archangel/Angel (Warren Worthington III), Banshee (Sean Cassidy), Beak (Barnell Bohusk), Cable (Nathan Summers), Cannonball (Sam Guthrie), Joanna Cargill, Chamber (Jono Starsmore), Changeling (Kevin Sidney), Tom Corsi, Cypher (Doug Ramsey), Dark Beast (Henry McCoy), Dazzler (Alison Blaire), Dust (Sooraya Qadir), E.V.A., Fantomex, Forearm, Forge, Sharon Friedlander, Husk (Paige Guthrie), Irina, Joseph, Jubilee (Jubilation Lee), Juggernaut (Cain Marko), Karma (Xi'an Coy Manh), Legion (David Haller), Lifeguard (Heather Cameron), Longneck, Longshot, Moira MacTaggart, Maggott (Japheth), Magik (Illyana Rasputin), Magma (Amara Aquilla), Magneto (Magnus), Marrow (Sarah), Marvel Girl/Phoenix (Jean Grey), Mimic (Calvin Rankin), Mirage/Moonstar (Dani Moonstar), Northstar (Jean-Paul Beaubier), Omerta (Paulie Provenzano), Phoenix Force, Professor X (Charles Xavier), Revanche, Cecilia Reyes, Sabretooth (Victor Creed), Sage (Tessa), Amanda Sefton (Magik), Slipstream (Davis Cameron), Stacy X (Miranda Leevald), Stepford Cuckoos (Phoebe, Celeste & Mindee), Alysande Stuart, Sunder, Sunfire (Shiro Yoshida), Sunpyre (Leyu Yoshida), Sunspot (Roberto da Costa), Thunderbird (John Proudstar), Thunderbird (Neal Shaara), Warlock, Wolfsbane (Rahne Sinclair), Wolverine imposter, Wraith (Hector Rendoza), X-Man (Nate Grey), Xorn (Kuan-Yin Xorn), Xorn (Shen Xorn)

BASE OF OPERATIONS: Xavier Institute for Higher Learning, Westchester, New York; formerly Reaver's base, Northern Territory, Australia; Mutant Research Center, Muir Island, Scotland; Magneto's Island, Bermuda Triangle

FIRST APPEARANCE: X-Men #1 (1963)

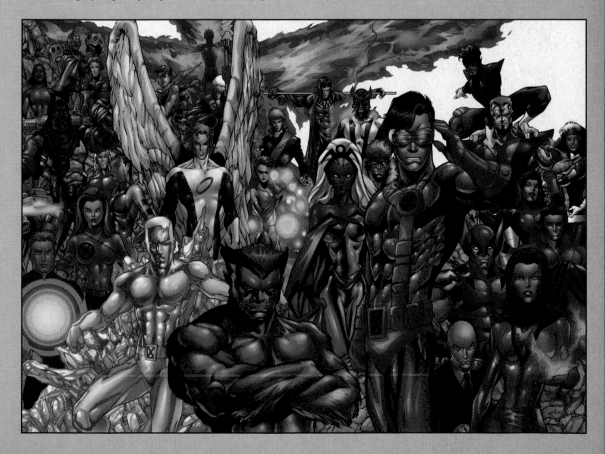

Art by Carlos Pacheco

mutant slave-runner Krueger, the criminal Dazzler (Angel's uncle, Burt Worthington), the telepathic alliance known as the Promise, the Inhuman Yeti, and the Secret Empire.

When the sentient island Krakoa captured most of his students, Xavier hastily assembled a second squad of X-Men. Traveling the world, he recruited Nightcrawler in Germany, Wolverine in Canada, Banshee in Ireland, Storm in Kenya, Sunfire in Japan, Colossus in Russia, and Thunderbird in America. Led by Cyclops, these all-new, all-different X-Men were able to rescue their predecessors. Except for Cyclops, the previous members all quit the expanded team. Sunfire also left the group, and Thunderbird died battling Count Nefaria and his Ani-Men during an attempted takeover of the N.O.R.A.D. facility in Cheyenne Mountain.

When the U.S. government unleashed new-model Sentinels that imprisoned Jean Grey and several other X-Men on a space station, the team escaped to Earth in a shuttle through a lethal solar-radiation storm. Dying from radiation, Jean was touched by the cosmic Phoenix Force, which replicated Jean's form and absorbed a portion of her consciousness. Guiding the shuttle to a crash-landing, the Phoenix Force secretly placed the real Jean in stasis within a cocoon-like pod at the bottom of Jamaica Bay, then took her place in the X-Men. The X-Men subsequently battled the Juggernaut, Magneto, Emperor D'Ken of the intergalactic Shi'ar Empire, the eccentric assassin Arcade, the prehistoric mutant Sauron, Alpha Flight, the reality-altering Proteus, and the Hellfire Club. The Club's probationary member Jason Wyngarde (Mastermind) mentally manipulated the Phoenix, who was rapidly corrupted by her own vast power and, as a result, transformed into Dark Phoenix. Ultimately, Jean's psyche resurfaced and convinced the Phoenix Force to sacrifice itself to save the universe. Believing Jean to be dead, Cyclops quit the team, leaving Storm to lead them in his absence.

The X-Men soon welcomed more new members, including Kitty Pryde, Rogue, and Rachel Summers. When the X-Men were believed dead after an encounter with the alien Brood, Xavier formed a new team of students dubbed the New Mutants. After the X-Men returned, Xavier continued to mentor both teams. The New Mutants even served temporarily as X-Men to save the team from interdimensional media mogul Mojo.

The real Jean Grey eventually revived and was reunited with the original X-Men members. Together they established X-Factor, supposedly a business dedicated to hunting and capturing dangerous mutants, but secretly a group formed to protect, recruit and mentor mutants in need of guidance, like Xavier before them. At the same time, the X-Factor group moonlighted as an openly mutant super-hero team, the X-Terminators. Their ranks already scattered and depleted after battles with the likes of Mr. Sinister's Marauders, the X-Men seemingly died battling the Adversary in Dallas, but they secretly survived and relocated to the Australian Outback, battling threats such as the cyborg Reavers, the Master Mold, and Nanny and her Orphan-Maker. While seeking the missing X-Men, Forge and Banshee helped form an ad-hoc team of X-Men to defend Muir Island from the Reavers. This team then fell under the thrall of the psychic Shadow King, and it took the combined efforts of the X-Men and X-Factor to defeat him. Afterwards, the members of X-Factor rejoined the X-Men which then split into two teams, Blue and Gold.

When Magneto nearly killed Wolverine by forcibly extracting the Adamantium implants from his skeleton, Xavier retaliated by telepathically lobotomizing Magneto; but Xavier paid a high price for this action. Tainted by Magneto's essence, Xavier unwittingly created the evil psionic entity Onslaught, which seemingly slew most of New York's major super heroes before being defeated. The heroes eventually returned, but not before Xavier was arrested for his part in the creation of Onslaught. Incarcerated, Xavier was interrogated by the hybrid Sentinel Bastion, who used the information he gained to launch an assault on the X-Men under the guise of the government-sponsored Operation: Zero Tolerance program. After the program was shut down, Xavier was forced to flee from his own mutant-locating computer Cerebro, which had become a sentient nanotech construct due to Bastion's machinations. Trying to realize Xavier's dream and fulfill its mutant-recruitment programming, Cerebro created solid holographic amalgamations of mutants in Xavier's files, then set about "recruiting" them to join a new team of X-Men with itself as their "founder." Cerebro's plan was foiled by the true X-Men, and it was ultimately stopped after Xavier caused it to overload.

Magneto soon resurfaced, holding the planet hostage with its own magnetic field, and convinced the world's leaders to grant him sovereignty over Genosha, an island nation near South Africa where humans once enslaved mutants. At first forced to cope with civil war and the effects of the lethal Legacy Virus, Magneto gained the might of a unified nation when a cure for the mutant plague was released into the atmosphere. Magneto proclaimed his intended dominance over mankind, standing ready to unleash an entire nation of mutates upon the planet. With the aid of a hastily-assembled interim team, the X-Men narrowly averted the would-be conqueror's ultimate offensive.

When Xavier and the X-Men were publicly outed as mutants by Xavier's genetic twin, Cassandra Nova, the Xavier Institute was overwhelmed with an influx of young mutants seeking safety and education. To cope with the large student body, Xavier recruited several new faculty members into the Institute, including former Alpha Flight member Northstar and a reformed Juggernaut. Xavier also formed the X-Corporation, a global search-and-rescue unit for oppressed mutants. The X-Corporation boasts headquarters around the world, with numerous mutants from the various splinter teams rallying to join the cause.

Following an all-out assault on Manhattan by a mutant posing as Magneto, which was opposed by another ad-hoc team of X-Men until the full team was reunited to thwart the villain, Xavier left the X-Men to help the true Magneto rebuild Genosha after it was devastated by a Sentinel attack. Cyclops and Emma Frost became co-headmasters of the Institute and reorganized the X-Men into three separate teams, leading one team themselves in an effort to improve the X-Men's standing with the public. A second team is led by Cyclops' brother Havok, while the third, the X-Treme Sanctions Executive led by Storm, acts as a global mutant police force.

PROFESSOR X
(Charles Xavier)
Founder in X-Men #42 (1967); not currently a member

NIGHTCRAWLER
(Kurt Wagner)
Joined in Giant-Size X-Men #1 (1975); current team leader

CYCLOPS
(Scott Summers)
Joined in X-Men #42 (1967); current co-headmaster & team leader

WOLVERINE
(James Howlett)
Joined in Giant-Size X-Men #1 (1975); current member of Cyclops' team

ICEMAN
(Robert 'Bobby' Drake)
Joined in X-Men #46 (1968); current member of Havok's team

BANSHEE
(Sean Cassidy)
Joined in Giant-Size X-Men #1 (1975); not currently a member

BEAST
(Henry 'Hank' McCoy)
Joined in X-Men #53 (1969); current member of Cyclops' team

STORM
(Ororo Munroe)
Joined in Giant-Size X-Men #1 (1975); not currently a member

ARCHANGEL
(Warren Worthington III)
Joined as Angel in X-Men #56 (1969); active as Archangel in X-Men #1 (1991); not currently a member

SUNFIRE
(Shiro Yoshida)
Joined in Giant-Size X-Men #1 (1975); not currently a member

JEAN GREY
(Jean Grey-Summers)
Joined as Marvel Girl in X-Men #1 (1963); active as Jean Grey in X-Men #1 (1991); active as Phoenix in Uncanny X-Men #318 (1994); not currently a member

COLOSSUS
(Piotr Rasputin)
Joined in Giant-Size X-Men #1 (1975); current member of Cyclops' team

MIMIC
(Calvin Rankin)
Joined in X-Men #27 (1966); not currently a member

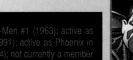
THUNDERBIRD
(James Proudstar)
Joined in Giant-Size X-Men #1 (1975); died in X-Men #95 (1975)

CHANGELING
(Kevin Sidney)
Active as Professor X in X-Men #40 (1968); died in X-Men #42 (1968)

PHOENIX FORCE
(Inapplicable)
Active as Phoenix in X-Men #101 (1976); physical form destroyed in X-Men #137 (1980)

POLARIS
(Lorna Dane)
Joined as Lorna Dane in X-Men #60 (1969); active as Magnetrix in X-Men: The Hidden Years #3 (2000); active as Polaris in Uncanny X-Men #428 (2004); current member of Havok's team

SHADOWCAT
(Katherine 'Kitty' Pryde)
Joined as Kitty in X-Men #138 (1980); active as Sprite in X-Men #139 (1980); active as Ariel in Marvel Graphic Novel #5 (1982); active as Shadowcat in Kitty Pryde & Wolverine #5 (1985); current member of Cyclops' team

HAVOK
(Alexander Summers)
Joined in X-Men #65 (1970); current team leader

LOCKHEED
Joined in Uncanny X-Men #166 (1983); current member of Cyclops' team

ROGUE
(Anna Marie, last name unrevealed)
Joined in Uncanny X-Men #171 (1983); current
member of Havok's team

REVANCHE
(Kwannon)
Joined in X-Men #21 (1993); died in X-Men #31
(1994)

RACHEL SUMMERS
(Rachel Grey)
Joined as Rachel in Uncanny X-Men #188 (1984); active
as Phoenix in Uncanny X-Men Annual #9 (1985); active
as Marvel Girl in Uncanny X-Men #444 (2004); current
member of Nightcrawler's team

CANNONBALL
(Samuel Guthrie)
Joined in X-Force #44 (1995); current member of
Nightcrawler's team

MAGNETO
(Unrevealed)
Headmaster of Xavier Institute in Uncanny
X-Men #200 (1985); active in Uncanny X-Men
#202 (1986); not currently a member

DARK BEAST
(Henry 'Hank' McCoy of Earth-295)
Active as Beast in X-Men Unlimited #10 (1996);
not currently a member

PSYLOCKE
(Elizabeth 'Betsy' Braddock)
Joined in Uncanny X-Men #213 (1987); current
member of Nightcrawler's team

JOSEPH
Joined in Uncanny X-Men #338 (1996); died in
X-Men #87 (1999)

DAZZLER
(Alison Blaire)
Joined in Uncanny X-Men #214 (1987); not
currently a member

CECILIA REYES
Joined in X-Men #70 (1997); not currently a
member

LONGSHOT
Joined in Uncanny X-Men #215 (1987); not currently
a member

MARROW
(Sarah)
Joined in X-Men #70 (1997); not currently a
member

FORGE
Joined in Uncanny X-Men #255 (1989); not currently
a member

MAGGOTT
(Japheth)
Joined in X-Men #70 (1997); died in Weapon X #5
(2002)

GAMBIT
(Remy LeBeau)
Joined in Uncanny X-Men Annual #14 (1990);
current member of Havok's team

WOLVERINE IMPOSTER
Active in Uncanny X-Men #371 (1999); died in
Astonishing X-Men #3 (1999)

JUBILEE
(Jubilation Lee)
Joined in Uncanny X-Men #273 (1991); not
currently a member

THUNDERBIRD
(Neal Shaara)
Joined in X-Men Unlimited #27 (2000); not
currently a member

BISHOP
(Lucas Bishop)
Joined in Uncanny X-Men #287 (1992); current
member of Nightcrawler's team

CABLE
(Nathan Summers)
Active in X-Men Unlimited #27 (2000); not
currently a member

MIRAGE
(Danielle Moonstar)
Active as Moonstar in X-Men #102 (2000); current faculty member

SAGE
(Tessa)
Active as Tessa in X-Men #102 (2000); active as Sage in X-Men #109 (2001); not currently a member

EMMA FROST
Joined in New X-Men #116 (2001); current co-headmaster & member of Cyclops' team

XORN
(Kuan-Yin Xorn)
Joined in New X-Men 2001 Annual (2001); died in New X-Men #150 (2003)

CHAMBER
(Jonothon Starsmore)
Joined in Uncanny X-Men #398 (2001); not currently a member

STACY X
(Miranda Leevald)
Joined in Uncanny X-Men #400 (2001); not currently a member

LIFEGUARD
(Heather Cameron)
Active in X-Treme X-Men #10 (2002); not currently a member

SLIPSTREAM
(Davis Cameron)
Active in X-Treme X-Men #10 (2002); not currently a member

NORTHSTAR
(Jean-Paul Beaubier)
Joined in Uncanny X-Men #414 (2002); not currently a member

HUSK
(Paige Guthrie)
Active in Uncanny X-Men #421 (2003); not currently a member

JUGGERNAUT
(Cain Marko)
Joined in Uncanny X-Men #425 (2003); not currently a member

XORN
(Shen Xorn)
Joined in X-Men #162 (2004); not currently a member

AD-HOC X-MEN ROSTERS

NEW MUTANT GRADUATE X-MEN
(Cannonball, Moonstar, Karma, Sunspot, Cypher, Warlock, Magma, Magik/Illyana Rasputin, Wolfsbane)
Formed in Uncanny X-Men Annual #10 (1986)

MUIR ISLAND X-MEN/MUIR ISLANDERS
(Banshee, Forge, Moira MacTaggart, Amanda Sefton, Sunder, Legion/David Haller, Sharon Friedlander, Tom Corsi, Alysande Stuart, Polaris, Multiple Man, Siryn)
Formed in Uncanny X-Men #254 (1989) until X-Factor Annual #6 (1991)

PHALANX COVENANT X-MEN
(Banshee, Jubilee, Sabretooth, Emma Frost)
Formed in Uncanny X-Men #316 (1994) until X-Men #37 (1994)

ASTONISHING X-MEN
(Cyclops, Phoenix/Jean Grey-Summers, Archangel, Cable, X-Man/Nate Grey, Wolverine Imposter)
Formed in Astonishing X-Men #1 (1999) until Astonishing X-Men #3 (1999)

GENOSHAN ASSAULT X-MEN
(Phoenix/Jean Grey-Summers, Northstar, Omerta/Paulie Provenzano, Wraith/Hector Rendoza, Sunpyre/Leyu Yoshida, Frenzy/Joanna Cargill, Dazzler)
Formed in Uncanny X-Men #392 (2001) until X-Men #113 (2001)

STREET TEAM X-MEN
(Cyclops, Fantomex, E.V.A., Stepford Cuckoos, Beak, Dust, Longneck, Forearm, Irina, other unnamed Xavier's students)
Formed in New X-Men #149 (2004) until New X-Men #150

XAVIER INSTITUTE FACULTY
(Mirage/Danielle Moonstar, Karma/Xi'an Coy Manh, Wolfsbane/Rahne Sinclair, Magma/Amara Aquilla)
Joined in New Mutants #2, New Mutants #4 (2003), New Mutants #11 (2004) & New X-Men: Academy X #15 (2005)

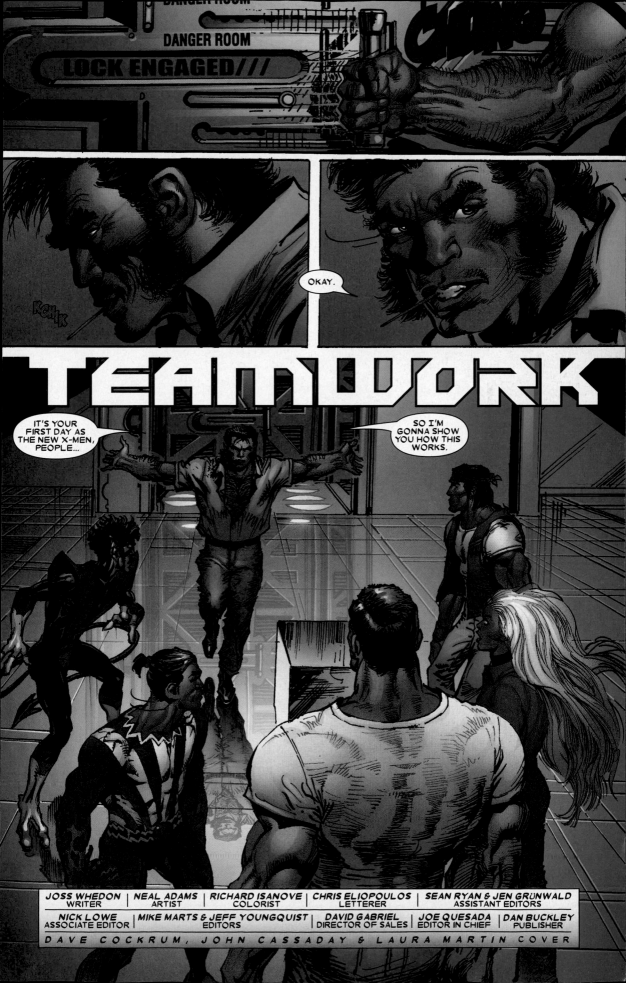

TEAMWORK

JOSS WHEDON | NEAL ADAMS | RICHARD ISANOVE | CHRIS ELIOPOULOS | SEAN RYAN & JEN GRUNWALD
WRITER | ARTIST | COLORIST | LETTERER | ASSISTANT EDITORS

NICK LOWE | MIKE MARTS & JEFF YOUNGQUIST | DAVID GABRIEL | JOE QUESADA | DAN BUCKLEY
ASSOCIATE EDITOR | EDITORS | DIRECTOR OF SALES | EDITOR IN CHIEF | PUBLISHER

DAVE COCKRUM, JOHN CASSADAY & LAURA MARTIN COVER

INCREDIBLE!
AN HOUR AGO I SPOKE NOT A WORD OF ENGLISH. NOW I UNDERSTAND EVERY WORD!

THE PROFESSOR IS A POWERFUL MAN.

I WOULD GLADLY UNLEARN ENGLISH IF I KNEW WHAT BANAL PRATTLE I'D ENDURE!

I ONLY JOINED THIS TEAM TO BE AMONG THE POWERFUL AND THE RIGHTEOUS, TO DO GREAT DEEDS THAT THE WORLD WOULD...

THAT...

WEREN'T WE SUPPOSED TO WEAR OUR COSTUMES?

THE LITTLE GERMAN IS WEARING HIS...

WRONG ON EVERY COUNT, SUNFLOWER.

SUNFIRE, YOU BRAINLESS--

WE'RE GOING TO GET COSTUMES?

WRONG HOW, WOLVERINE?

CALLED US A TEAM.

WHICH WE AIN'T.

THE BOISTEROUS, BELLIGERENT BEGINNING!

CAT-5 WINDS, BETTER THAN 200 KNOTS, DRIVING RAIN SO HARD IT HURTS.

STAN LEE PRESENTS

FINDING HOME!

BY CHRIS CLAREMONT & RICK LEONARDI

JOHN PROUDSTAR CAN'T SEE HIS ADVERSARY, HE CAN BARELY STAND...

...BUT HE DOESN'T QUIT.

SOONER OR LATER, HE'LL FIND STORM.

JIMMY PALMIOTTI INKER	PAUL MOUNTS COLORS	VC'S JOE CARAMAGNA LETTERS	SALVADOR LARROCA COVER	JENNIFER GRUNWALD, SEAN RYAN & MICHAEL SHORT ASSISTANT EDITORS
NICK LOWE & MARK BEAZLEY ASSOCIATE EDITORS	MIKE MARTS & JEFF YOUNGQUIST EDITORS	DAVID GABRIEL DIRECTOR OF SALES	JOE QUESADA EDITOR IN CHIEF	DAN BUCKLEY PUBLISHER

AND WHEN HE DOES...

THAT'S ENOUGH, STORM.

LET'S MOVE ON.

EXCELLENT CONTROL OVER THE WEATHER. NONE OF US WATCHING FELT A DROP.

NEXT ROUND, ENGAGE WITHOUT POWERS.

YO, ONE-EYE, I DON'T FIGHT GIRLS.

KICKS LIKE A MULE, HE THINKS.

BUT SO DID UNCLE JACK, WHO TAUGHT HIM HOW TO FIGHT.

QUICKER THAN EXPECTED.

OH GREAT--AND SNEAKY, TOO.

HER FIRST MISTAKE.

IMPACT WOULD'A FINISHED ANYONE THIS SIDE OF THE WOLVERINE.

HE TAKES IT IN STRIDE.

IMPORTANT THING IS FOR HER TO GRAB HIM WITH HER CLOAK...

...MEANS HE ALSO HAS HOLD OF HER.

HE KNOWS SQUAT ABOUT AFRICA, WHERE SHE COMES FROM.

BUT HIS PEOPLE ARE THE CHIRICAHUA APACHE.

NOBODY TOUGHER, OR MORE CUNNING, IN THE WORLD.

I SHOULD'A BEEN THE ONE TO *DIE.*

SHOULD'A BEEN ME, *UNCLE JACK.*

I SHOULD'A BEEN THE ONE TO SAVE *YOU.*

MS. *MUNROE--*

--IT'S ME, *JOHN PROUDSTAR.*

I JUST WANTED TO--

--WASTE MY TIME, NOBODY'S HOME.

TALK ABOUT TRAVELLIN' *LIGHT.*

GEEZ-- *PROFESSOR--!*

YOU STRUCK A VERY *RAW* NERVE.

"DAMAGED GOODS."

SOMETHING LIKE THAT.

MERELY A TELEPATHIC PROJECTION, JOHN.

THAT'S WHY SHE REACTED AS SHE DID DURING YOUR EXERCISE.

ORORO USED THAT *KNIFE* TO *KILL* A MAN, WHEN SHE WAS HARDLY MORE THAN A CHILD.

IT'S HER GREATEST *SECRET.*

I DON'T TELL TALES, SIR. HERS--OR *YOURS.*

EATON
HILLSMAN II!
D'ARMATA